CATHOLICISM AND AMERICA

Faith and Reason: Studies in Catholic Theology and Philosophy

The series aims at publishing scholarly studies that serve the project of "faith seeking understanding." We hope to assist in making available in English valuable work being done by theologians and philosophers abroad; in this regard we recognize a special place for the ongoing renaissance in Thomistic theology and philosophy. In addition to translations, we intend to publish collections of essays and monographs from a range of perspectives, united by their common commitment to the ecclesial and sapiential work of "faith seeking understanding" so as to build up the Church and proclaim the Gospel afresh.

Published Volumes

Serge-Thomas Bonino, OP, ed., *Surnaturel: Reflections on Nature and Grace*
Gilles Emery, OP, *Trinity, Church, and the Human Person: Thomistic Essays*
Lawrence Feingold, *The Natural Desire to See God*
Matthew L. Lamb, *Eternity, Time, and the Life of Wisdom*
Guy Mansini, OSB, *The Word Has Dwelt Among Us*
Thomas Joseph White, OP, *Wisdom in the Face of Modernity*
Adrian J. Reimers, *Truth about the Good: John Paul II on Moral Norms*
Lawrence J. Welch, *The Presence of Christ in the Church*
Matthew L. Lamb, ed., *Catholicism and America: Challenges and Prospects*

CATHOLICISM AND AMERICA: CHALLENGES AND PROSPECTS

Fr. Matthew L. Lamb, Editor

Sapientia Press
of Ave Maria University

Sapientia Press
of Ave Maria University
5050 Ave Maria Blvd.
Ave Maria, FL 34142
888–343–8607

Cover Design: Eloise Anagnost

Cover Photo: Larry Brownstein/Photodisc/Getty Images

Printed in the United States of America.

Library of Congress Control Number: 2012945595

ISBN: 978-1-932589-63-4

Contents

Introduction

POPES JOHN PAUL II and Benedict XVI have emphasized the need for contemporary societies to cultivate intellectual commitments to truth and wisdom, along with moral virtues fostering good and noble citizens. Such wisdom and goodness are fundamental to the dignity of human persons and the flourishing of human communities. Catholic intellectual traditions offer enormous resources on the importance of intellectual and moral virtues. These traditions are not peculiar to Catholics. As the recent Popes have insisted, these traditions are open to all, thanks to man's God-given intelligence and reason. There is a resurgent interest in "virtue ethics." Yet Americans tend to limit virtues to private individual morality.

The contributions to this volume argue for a fuller understanding of the contributions Catholicism can make to the United States of America during the twenty-first century. Some were initially presented during a conference at Ave Maria University. All the presentations go behind the headlines portraying Catholic opposition to contraception, homosexual acts, same-sex marriage, abortion, euthanasia, human embryonic stem cell research, and other so-called hot button issues. Rarely do media cover what Pope Benedict XVI calls the "dictatorship of relativism" that threatens any and all contemporary societies and cultures, undermining foundations for a reasoned practice of religious freedom, tolerance, and democracy.

The essays in this volume explore these deeper threats to society and culture along with the contributions that Catholic perspectives provide for meeting those threats. The first set of chapters in part 1 indicates some of the main threats to American culture from its inadequate post-Enlightenment biases. In doing this these chapters also indicate the resources in Catholic traditions for integrating human reason and science with Christian faith and wisdom. Part 2 then takes up the contributions to the American experiment in the Catholic theological work of Fr. John Courtney Murray, S.J. What is a proper understanding and practice of religious liberty, and how is it in jeopardy today? The chapters in part 3 take up the need for a vibrant Catholic intellectual and religious identity in Catholic higher education in the United States.

Francis Cardinal George, O.M.I., Archbishop of Chicago, draws upon the documents of the Second Vatican Council (Vatican II) and of Pope Benedict XVI to spell out how the Council actually preserved and deepened the fundamental principles of Catholic teachings by changing the applications of those principles. The separation of church and state, the Cardinal points out, has its institutional and moral dimensions in deeper cultural and anthropological issues revealed in the transcendence of the kingdom of God over all earthly kingdoms. The Cardinal indicates the important change brought about by the Council in responding from Christian faith to the modern world.

Caesar is not God, as Pope Benedict indicates when citing the witness of the Christian martyrs to the transcendence (and so transpolitical reality) of Christ in glory. The reforms of Vatican II combine the continuity of tradition in the principles of faith with the discontinuity of the new situations defined by modern sciences, modern states, and dialogues among the world religions. The secularization of the state does not mean the same as a secularized culture in which the truths of faith and moral virtues are excluded. Indeed, as Cardinal George indicates, such a totally secularized culture cannot sustain a vibrant democracy, given its dehumanizing relativism and nihilism. The Cardinal emphasizes the limitations of democracy and its authority. The Catholic Church, founded by the Incarnate Son of God, Jesus Christ, and his chosen apostles and their successors down the ages, transcends all the political regimes of this world, including the political regime of the United States.

Fr. Matthew Lamb traces a root of the problems in America today to a failure to promote the practice of the virtues of reasoned judgment, that is, the virtues of theoretical and practical wisdom. These virtues were replaced by technology, social engineering, and a scientism that hands all of human and cultural life over to a techno-scientism unable to discern what is genuinely human. Mass media with its public opinion polls promotes this tendency toward a lowering of standards in the name of equal rights for all, irrespective of good or evil, virtue or vice. To appreciate Catholicism one needs to explore the two millennial developments of its intellectual and theological traditions.

Father Lamb sketches a few major developments: the first millennium of Catholicism could be called the patristic, conciliar, and monastic millennium. Having witnessed the collapse of the great Greco-Roman cultures, the Greek and Latin Fathers of the Church saw the importance of cultivating the intellectual life within communities dedicated as well to the quests for wisdom and holiness. From the revelation in the book of Genesis, they saw how man's God-given reason—what was highest and most godlike in him—could lead to a prideful, disordered desire to be like God. So the great intellectual achievements of the classical world were preserved in the monastic, cathedral, and convent schools.

The second millennium saw the emergence of the universities out of the cathedral schools. These new institutions emphasized science and scholarship; concerns were raised that if these were divorced from the quest for wisdom and holiness, pride could again derail such intelligence into the service of dominative power—the "libido dominandi" that St. Augustine saw as an effect of original sin. The spread of nominalism and voluntarism from the works of Duns Scotus and William Ockham throughout the Reformation and Enlightenment solidified the divorce of science and scholarship from acquired metaphysical wisdom, as well as from faith and wisdom and holiness. As the millennium came to an end in world wars and the dead ends of the Holocaust, genocides, and massive abortion infanticides, Popes John Paul II and Benedict XVI emphasized the third millennial challenge for Catholicism to free reason from the dictatorship of relativism and nihilism, and to begin the task of finding new ways of integrating science, scholarship, and the arts with the quests for wisdom and holiness. Indeed, Pope Benedict saw the fateful conjunction in our time of Western nominalism with Islamic voluntarism so evident in the terrorist violence waged by both nations and Jihadist groups.

Peter Lawler explores the philosophical and theological roots of the challenges Catholicism poses to the nominalism in American culture. He is a scholar whose publications have uncovered many cultural antinomies resulting from the pervasive effects of nominalism on the Enlightenment thinkers who have influenced modern democracies. Drawing on the writings of Pope Benedict XVI, Lawler sketches the replacement of the quest for wisdom with the desire for manipulative power; the integral whole of life is replaced with free-floating individuals cut loose from family and community responsibilities. The will to power eclipses a wise attunement to the whole of nature; laws are no longer acts of reason but arbitrary acts of those in power. Invoking Murray's comment that the Founders of the American republic "built better than they knew," Lawler emphasizes the importance of the revelation of the Triune God personalizing the Divine and overcoming the impersonal abstractions of classical natural theology as well as the modern abstractions of a Darwinism that sabotages personal dignity. Against libertarians, Darwinians, and Evangelicals, Lawler sees the importance of the science of theology integrating human reason and divine faith. Hellenic Christianity transformed European cultures that were influenced by classical philosophy.

Following Pope Benedict, Lawler sees the recovery of Trinitarian theology as a science able to counteract the baneful effects of modern nominalism in America. Theological science seeks an understanding of the faith that links explanations to wisdom. It would collaborate in overcoming the detachment of persons from nature. In attuning human minds and hearts to the whole of reality as created and redeemed by the Triune God, it would replace the historicism and materialism that set up "the state of nature" doomed to violence and a war of all against all. Lawler concludes by reflecting that what we Americans need is not less but more science: Pope Benedict XVI points us in the direction of the theory, culminating in the science of theology, adequate to the great success of the experiment in freedom of our political founders. The Greek and Latin Fathers of the Church, as Pope Benedict states, knew how to take up the philosophical achievements of their classical predecessors into a Hellenic Catholicism. Socrates, Plato, Aristotle, Cicero—these founders of classical cultures also built better than they knew. Trinitarian theology initiated the development of the notions of person relative to nature. Thus a science of theology would enable the human sciences to understand how the prevalence of violence in human life is not due to "a state of nature" but to the depersonalization of sin and evil.

Daniel J. Mahoney reflects on the mutations that the theological-political problem has undergone recently. Drawing upon the writings of Pierre Manent he is able to offer corrections both to the secularist rejection of God and to a too facile reduction of Christian faith to an ethics of rights espoused by liberalism. Catholicism cannot succumb to the privatization of religion and faith. In an aside during the conference, Cardinal George mentioned that he plans on writing a book entitled *What Can God Do in Public?* Mahoney provides important elements in answering that question. Fundamentally it means overcoming the eclipse of truth in matters of morality and religion. Just as Lawler calls for a science of theology to mediate the truth of Catholic faith to American culture, so Mahoney indicates the need for the Church to proclaim that truth for the sake of a genuine "liberty under God" that realizes that Christianity is not "essentially" capable of being identical with democracy—the Church founded by the Incarnate Son of God is not democratic—but rather seeks a "prudential accommodation" with democracy, as it does with all political regimes. This is the task Vatican II has set for the Church during the third millennium.

Mahoney concludes with the sharp choice we face today: "[W]e can conceive man as sovereign Lord of existence, the autonomous creator of his own 'values,' or we can see in him a being who participates in a natural order that he did not make, an 'order of things' that gives meaning to his freedom and that makes sense of his search for truth."

Marc Guerra explores further the perspectives opened by Lawler and Mahoney, and relates them to Lamb's analysis of the resources Catholicism has in the works of St. Augustine and St. Thomas Aquinas. In taking both Catholicism and democracy seriously, Guerra spells out the consequences of nominalism and Enlightenment replacement of virtue with technology. Guerra contrasts Mahoney's position on a chastened liberalism with those who see the old-fashioned liberalism of the America founding as totally, and not just prudentially, compatible with Christianity. Guerra spells out the transpolitical character of the Christian faith that finds the concrete dignity of individuals and their quest for genuine justice fulfilled only in the eternal, transpolitical City of God. As Guerra states,

> Given modernity's inherent desire to resolve the theologico-political problem, Christian political thought today must renew its appreciation of Augustine's teaching on the distinction between the earthly city and the City of God. Because it does not absolutize politics, Augustine's doctrine of the two cities avoids the monadic temptations of ideological totalitarianism and theocratic despotism. By drawing sharp lines between the temporal and the eternal, and the political and the spiritual, Augustine calls attention to the fact that politics is an inherently limited enterprise and that man ultimately longs for a form of wholeness that transcends the political order.

Archbishop Charles Chaput introduces part 2 by dealing with the important contributions of Fr. John Courtney Murray, S.J., to serious reflection on Catholicism and American democracy. Archbishop Chaput takes up the problems the essays in part 1 sketched in late modernity rooted in a lack of attention to virtue in America's late republic. He graphically outlines the problems we face and returns to Murray's writing to indicate how often his work was misunderstood as compromising Catholicism for the sake of democracy. Quite the contrary, as the Archbishop indicates.

This is further elaborated in the article by George Weigel. His chapter indicates the cultural and epistemological achievements of the work of Fr. John Courtney Murray's reflections on the American proposition. Weigel indicates that Murray's assessment of the United States and its polity was not dependent on Thomas Hobbes or John Locke, with their mistaken notions of the state of nature as radically conflictual. Instead, Murray drew upon more classical and Catholic understandings of human nature as ordered to the truth and the good. The American proposition as Murray presented it rested upon four truths: (1) The nation is under the transcendent judgment of God, whose natural law instills the need for all human beings to live by what is highest in themselves, the common good directing their intelligence and reason. (2) Hence, consent of the governed means, for Murray, that the dignity of human persons demands that they engage in intelligent and reasoned debate pursuant to the common good of their persons, families, regions, societies. (3) This means that, for Murray, society takes priority over the state, which is in the service of the common good of the society. Catholic teaching insists upon the principle of subsidiarity: the state should not usurp the responsibilities of the family, the community, or the corporation. (4) Freedom will flourish only if citizens are virtuous. Legislation requires sound practical judgments if the laws are to foster genuine intellectual and moral excellence or virtue.

Bad habits or vices contract and constrict human freedom; anyone addicted to disordered desires is not free to enjoy truly the good he desires; addictions engender despondency and despair. Good habits or virtues expand human freedom and the pursuit of genuine happiness. Weigel then concludes with a trenchant analysis of the challenges we are facing today in the light of this analysis by Murray, especially in the light of the cultural dictatorship of relativism and the antilife nihilism of decadence. Weigel ends with a warning by Murray of the perils we face.

Michael Novak's response to George Weigel's reflections indicates the importance of recognizing the dangers of "soft nihilism" in American culture, while he also defends Murray's contributions against some of their theological and philosophical critics. He then sketches three more truths that indicate the importance of the American experiment in democracy for our times.

The chapters in part 3 raise issues important for a renewal of genuine Catholic higher education. William Cardinal Levada, Prefect of the Congregation for the Doctrine of the Faith, introduces part 3 on Catholic higher education with a baccalaureate homily he gave at Ave Maria University on May 7, 2011. Higher education will be vibrantly Catholic insofar as it provides the intellectual and spiritual friendship with Jesus Christ. The Cardinal dramatically recounts the sufferings and failings in the long history of the Church. Catholic doctrinal and sacramental life on a university campus are to form students in a life of study and of prayer aimed at ever-deepening intimacy with Christ. Catholic faith does not weaken but strengthens the life of reason in its quest for truth and the will in its desire for the good. The Cardinal's homily emphasizes how faith and friendship with Jesus Christ as truly God and truly man enlightens human minds and hearts. Grace never destroys but perfects nature and the universe created by and in the Divine Word.

Thomas Hibbs explores the challenges facing Catholic higher education in America today. The universities and colleges are most important if the educational, health care, and pastoral achievements of Catholics in America are to communicate the distinctive Catholic contributions to the culture of the nation—a culture deeply influenced by advances in science, scholarship, and health care. Hibbs draws upon the insights of John Cardinal Newman, W. E. B. DuBois, John Tracy Ellis, Harry Lewis, and Alasdair MacIntyre to demonstrate the importance of a serious study of both the liberal arts and the sciences. Hibbs points out the dangers of reducing human reason, as some moderns did, to a calculating instrument in the pursuit of dominative power. Truly liberal education in the Catholic tradition will influence three key components in all higher education.

First, the selection of the faculty requires a discernment of their ability to excel in teaching and passing on the wisdom and science faithful to the great achievements of both the past and the present. Second, the curriculum has to foster the intellectual and moral excellence of both faculty and students. Here Hibbs shows the importance of Greek and Latin philosophers when engaging in contemporary questions and problems. Pope Benedict XVI has indicated the importance of ancient and medieval reflections on wisdom and truth for the cultivation of both mind and heart today. Hibbs sees the importance for American Catholic universities to realize what Pope Benedict in his Regensburg lecture calls "the inner rapprochement between Biblical revelation and Greek philosophical inquiry,"[1] and how that Hellenic discovery of reason influences the best of the Roman thinkers as well. Hibbs shows how Catholic intellectuals have not only misunderstood Msgr. Tracy Ellis's call for intellectual excellence. Just as Fr. John Courtney Murray's thought was distorted by those who invoked him in their efforts to secularize the Church, so some Catholics invoked Msgr. Ellis's work to justify their secularization of Catholic universities, thereby failing to uphold the Graeco-Roman heritage of rooting cultures in the high standards of intellectual and moral virtues. Finally, Hibbs calls attention to the need for Catholic universities to integrate the classroom with the dorm, education with student life. The compatibility

---

1 Pope Benedict XVI, "Faith, Reason and the University: Memories and Reflections" (lecture, University of Regensburg, Germany, September 12, 2006), sec. 29.

of reason and Catholic faith requires careful attention, not only to hiring and curriculum, but also to the sacramental and prayer life of the faculty and students.

Michael Dauphinais explores how higher education today is allergic to the truth in the realms of morality and religion. This is especially detrimental to Catholic institutions of higher education. Drawing on Pope John Paul II's *Ex Corde Ecclesiae* and *Fides et Ratio*, as well as the writings and statements of Pope Benedict XVI on both human and revealed truth, Dauphinais illustrates the dictatorship of relativism in the loss of Catholic identity, and the need for genuine education to open both faculty and students to formative influences of truth and goodness. He clarifies how the Hellenic and Latin emphasis on virtue is supported and elevated by the theological virtues, as Aquinas clearly taught.

The essays in this book are important and insightful contributions to a deeper understanding of the challenges and prospects Catholicism faces in the United States of America today. In a country and a world marked by secularization with deep roots in nominalism and the Reformation, as Brad S. Gregory demonstrates in his *The Unintended Reformation: How a Religious Revolution Secularized Society*, the essays here show how Roman Catholic faith and teachings clarify the God-given nature of reason common to every member of the human race. In a country and a world marked by religious pluralism, it is vitally important for Catholics in America to rise to the challenges the Catholic Magisterium set us in Vatican II, to move the dialogue of world religions toward reasoned truth in the context of a mutual search for wisdom, and away from the irrationality of violent dominative power.

Theologically, just as the Triune God is more intimate to each individual than that individual is even to himself, so also this incredible individual intimacy is universal. God loves each and every human being. In God each instant of each human being's life is present. No human empires can redeem the sufferings, tears, and blood shed each day of human history. Only the eternal loving presence of God, as revealed in Jesus' proclamation of the kingdom of God in his life, death, and resurrection is all human suffering and evil redeemed. Only God forgives the countless sins of the intelligent creatures he in his goodness creates and redeems.

The Catholic college and university need to recover the roles of philosophy and theology in an interdisciplinary collaboration with the natural and human sciences, with the liberal arts. Only the labors of universities over centuries will build up an architectonic wisdom open to, and integrative with, all real advances in science and scholarship. Catholic graduate programs in philosophy and theology should lead the way in reintegrating science, scholarship, and the humanities with wisdom and holiness.

If we are both faithful and intelligent, we may discover that the great Catholic intellectual traditions are, in fact, a vast and complex cathedral of the mind and heart to which each generation of human beings is called to contribute—a cathedral of the mind and heart, far more enduring than those of stone, wherein we can cultivate attentive reverence for the goodness and holiness of every real question, of every act of correct understanding, of every act of holy love. In such a cathedral of the mind and heart every genuine discovery is ultimately a gift, a finite, created participation in the wondrous, embracing mystery of Father, Son, and Holy Spirit: Infinite Understanding generating Infinite Wisdom spirating Infinite Love. For this cathedral of the mind and heart is the whole Body of Christ in the City of God.

PART 1

CATHOLICISM CHALLENGES AMERICAN CULTURE

CHAPTER 1

Continuity in Change: Catholicism and American Culture

FRANCIS CARDINAL GEORGE, O.M.I.
Archbishop of Chicago

THE INTERSECTION or relationship between Catholicism and American culture can be used to illustrate continuity in change. I will make use of what our Holy Father called the "hermeneutic of reform" when he gave a conference to the Roman Curia in the first year of his pontificate. That address inspired the book *Vatican II: Renewal within Tradition*, because Father Lamb and others wanted to show how within the theological discipline there could be continuity in change in understanding the teachings of the Second Vatican Council.[1] In a civic context, which is the relationship between Catholicism, our culture, and our government, there is also continuity in change, which simply means that both parties to the conversation are alive and contributing to it.

For those of you familiar with my book *The Difference God Makes*,[2] this theme features prominently throughout most of the chapters. The basic theme is ecclesial communion and its theological roots in participative metaphysics, particularly that of St. Thomas. If relationship is key to understanding the Church and is therefore key to our understanding of who we are as the Body of Christ, then theologians must explore the particularities of those relationships. We live through Christ, in Christ, and with Christ, as the priest proclaims at the end of the canon of the Mass.

---

1 See Matthew L. Lamb and Matthew Levering, eds., *Vatican II: Renewal within Tradition* (New York: Oxford University Press, 2008). The volume begins with Pope Benedict XVI's address on the proper hermeneutic for understanding Vatican II, pp. ix–xv.

2 Francis Cardinal George, O.M.I., *The Difference God Makes: A Catholic Vision of Faith, Communion, and Culture* (New York: Doubleday, 2009).

There is not a lot of exploration of what it means to live "through" someone, and I hope theologians will continue to deepen our understanding of the relations that connect the network of ecclesial communion.

I would like to take this occasion to develop in new directions, considering the Church's external relations to the world. If there is tension in the relationship between Catholicism and our culture, very often the tension is located in moral issues. I remember when I was studying religion as a high school student; our text spoke about differences between Protestants and Catholics and explained how the differences are doctrinal. There are no real differences, we were taught, between the moral teaching of Protestant churches and that of the Catholic Church. One could not say that today, and because this remains a predominantly Protestant country, the development of moral and social issues in ways that are in opposition to Catholic moral theology creates tensions not only between ourselves and ecumenical partners in our dialogues but also between a culture still predominantly shaped by Protestantism, even if it is a secularized Protestantism, and our own Catholicism. This difference surfaces when we get into disputes about the legal approval of killing the unborn, about the nature of marriage and family, and about problems around the prevalence of sexual promiscuity. But while real, this is not primarily what I want to consider in talking about Catholicism and American culture.

The tension between society and Catholicism is often expressed in constitutional terms—that is, as the separation of church and state. A major thesis in ecclesiology before the Second Vatican Council was that the state has the obligation to protect its citizens against error, particularly error in revealed religion, and therefore the state should recognize the Catholic religion, even though the state itself as a secular institution is not religious. The state was not to separate itself from religion but rather to embrace it in such a way that society itself would know the truth and could live in an upright way. That thesis was much contested because of our American experience, where we had freedom of religion without the union of church and state in any fashion, although the state was not unfriendly to religion. Government gave tax privileges and other such aids to religious expression; still, Americans before the Council were very uneasy with the received theological thesis about state-recognized religion. A well-known Jesuit theologian of the day, Fr. John Courtney Murray, who later became a peritus at the Second Vatican Council (Vatican II), wrote a series of articles in *Theological Studies* in the midfifties and then a book, *We Hold These Truths*, in which he said that the thesis might have been true in a state that had an obligation to regulate, to be present to, every dimension of human experience: a comprehensive state, perhaps even a totalitarian state. That was the notion of the state that the Magisterium of the Church was assuming, and, of course, in that situation the state must indeed protect its citizens from error, as it must protect its citizens from everything else.

Fr. Courtney Murray explained that that is the European perspective to which the Magisterium was referring, but that is not ours. In our constitutional order, we live in a limited state, and, therefore, there is a way to resolve theoretical tensions about the separation of church and state by pointing out that the state, in our American history and according to our U.S. Constitution, is fundamentally restricted in its outreach in human affairs. A limited state permits freedom by reducing its own grasp. It should encourage what is good but do so not directly through religion but rather according to natural moral law, which could be universally acceptable because we could reason to it. Fr. Courtney Murray's thesis was very well argued. Today, unfortunately, natural moral law has become a Catholic tag word. Bringing it up transforms any argument into a religious argument. Positive law is regarded as a function of will, and it provides the only normative social directives that we can all accept if we are going to continue to live together. Social norms are a matter of political negotiation, not based on appeals to right reason.

At Vatican II however, it was not Fr. Courtney Murray's original thesis that won the day in *Dignitatis Humanae*, the document on religious freedom. The Council used an anthropological analysis that was inspired as much by French personalism as it was by the American experience, although both worked hand in hand in creating the conciliar document. The Second Vatican Council spoke not about the nature of the state but about the nature of human freedom. It described the nature of religious assent as intrinsically free, something that can never be imposed, particularly by a secular authority. The tension between religion and society, therefore, is less a question of constitutional or legal order and more a cultural question. In the Magisterium of Pope John Paul II, church and state, and their relationship, do not take center stage. What is discussed is the relationship between faith and culture. The relationship is not an institutional question, nor is it even, first of all, a moral question; it is rather a cultural question, an anthropological question.

The Pope spoke often about enculturating the faith. In the conversation between faith and culture, cultures are always evangelically ambiguous but still good in themselves, just as human nature, while fallen, remains salvageable; it is good although wounded. One can find *semina verbi*, seeds of the Word, God's word, in any culture, and it is up to the faith and its evangelizers and missionaries to study a culture sympathetically and to live within it and find what is it that can be used in order to express the faith in it. Pope John Paul II did that vis-à-vis American culture when visiting Chicago in his first visit to this country after his election as Pope in 1979. He was in Chicago, at Grant Park next to the great Lake Michigan. Speaking to all the ethnic groups who were assembled there, speaking to all of those Catholics with roots in so many parts of the world, he referred to our national motto, e pluribus unum, "from many, one," to explain that, just as we have created something new here, and something that is truly good in the American union, so also St. Paul wrote in his epistles about creating the Body of Christ from many differences, individual and cultural and social, that were present where Paul evangelized. There are always *semina verbi*, the good elements in any culture.

Our own culture is constituted on ideas because we are not a nation of blood; first of all, we are a nation of choice. In what is created by choice there is something analogous to religious experience, religious conversion, and so we can use in religious expression our American habit of constructing a life on shared belief. But there comes a point in any culture, including our own, when you can no longer enculturate the faith, incarnate the truths of revealed religion, because the culture shows itself inimical to the faith. At that point, you have to convert the culture; you have to evangelize the culture. These are the two movements that the Pope spoke about in his new conversation between faith and culture: enculturate the faith and evangelize the culture. It's a dynamic familiar to parents raising children, isn't it? They find what is good because there is always something wonderful in every child; they encourage it, develop it, make it into what the parent knows is needed so that the child can flourish. But there is also self-righteousness and stubbornness and egotism and a meanness, even in little kids, that has to be changed, has to be converted, has to be evangelized, to use the theological term.

In the dialogue between faith and culture that is part of spreading the Gospel, we recognize that there is evangelization beyond individual conversion. The Church is called to be a leaven in society. The Council taught that all those called to holiness by reason of baptism are to prepare themselves for life eternal, and to transform the world. God so loved the world that he wants us to love it too and make it just a little bit more like the kingdom of God—more peaceful, more just, more charitable and loving. What are some obstacles to this mission for the Church in the United States?

The Catholic Church is essentially and by divine foundation (jus divinum), a fully *hierarchical* Church, whereas the foundational document of the United States of America, the Declaration of Independence, proclaims in ringing words that "all men are created equal." Of course it has always been a part of Church teaching that human persons are, without exception, *metaphysically* equal, and therefore equal before God. As St. Paul says in his Letter to the Romans, "God shows no partiality" (Romans 2:11).

Paul is speaking here in the context of salvation history. His central point is that the coming of Jesus Christ had, among other things, cast a retrospective light on the central fact of *past* salvation history, which from the Bible's point of view recognized the central division between the Chosen People of Israel and the Gentile (our own ancestors for the most part) "nations" who, while not entirely outside the pale of God's concerns, had yet to receive the light of revelation that had been given to the people of Israel. But with the coming of God's definitive revelation in Jesus Christ, Paul could demonstrate that, first, "all have sinned and fall short of the glory of God" (Romans 3:23) and, second, that all "are justified by his grace as a gift, through the redemption which is in Christ Jesus" (Romans 3:24).

Such statements nevertheless did not prevent Paul from claiming a unique *authority* over not only the churches he founded but even over a church, that of Rome, that he had yet to visit! Note the key word "revelation" here. Precisely because Paul received a revelation from God, he has an authority that comes with that revelation, a point he makes with special ferocity when that same authority is under challenge, as happened with the churches in Galatia: "Brethren, I would have you know," he says to the Galatians, "that the gospel which was preached by me is not man's gospel. For I did not receive it from man, nor was I taught it, but it came through a *revelation* of Jesus Christ" (Galatians 1:11–12; emphasis added). So also he begins his Letter to the Romans with that same claim: "Paul, a servant of Christ Jesus, called to be an apostle, set apart for the gospel of God" (Romans 1:1).

One reason that Karl Barth's famous commentary, *Epistle to the Romans*, so shocked the theological world in the years immediately following the First World War was because it marked a clean break from previous attempts of liberal Christianity (i.e., Christianity that tries always to only co-relate culture and faith and not also to challenge the culture when necessary) to downplay Paul's essentially *divine* authority. Although Barth later came to abandon some of the more extreme dialectical positions he adopted in his commentary on the Letter to the Romans, nonetheless his commentary on this first verse of Paul's Epistle bears quoting in full because it captures exactly the kind of unique claim that Paul is making to the Christians in Rome:

> Fashioned of the same stuff as all other men, a stone differing in no way from other stones, yet in his relation to God—and in this

> only—he is unique. As an apostle—and only as an apostle—he stands in no organic relationship with human society, as it exists in history: seen from the point of view of human society, he can be regarded only as an exception, nay, rather, as impossibility. Paul's position can be justified only as resting in God, and so only can his words be regarded as at all credible, for they are as incapable of direct apprehension as is God Himself. For this reason he dares to approach others and to demand a hearing without fear either of exalting himself or of approximating too closely to his audience. He appeals only to the authority of God. This is the ground of his authority. There is no other.[3]

We are here at some distance from John Paul II on the shores of Lake Michigan, looking for points of contact with American culture. I presume it can also go without saying that, in the American polity, authority can make no claim like Paul's. On the contrary, the whole point of the Declaration of Independence was to reject the authority of King George III and, by implication, any appeal to a putative *divine* right of kings to rule over the people they governed. The ringing words of the Declaration are famous enough, but perhaps they bear repeating just to see how much they differ in rhetorical style from Paul's justification of his authority:

> When in the course of human events it becomes necessary for one people to dissolve the political bands which have connected them with another, and to assume among the powers of the earth, the separate and *equal* station to which the Laws of Nature and of Nature's God *entitle* them, a decent respect to the opinions of mankind requires that they should declare the causes which impel them to the separation.—We hold these truths to be self-evident, that all men are created *equal,* that they are endowed by their Creator with certain unalienable Rights, that among these are Life, *Liberty*, and the pursuit of Happiness.—That to secure these rights, Governments are instituted among Men, *deriving their just powers from the consent of the governed,*—That whenever any Form of Government becomes destructive of these ends, it is the Right of the People to alter or to abolish it, and to institute [a] new Government, laying its foundation on such principles and organizing its powers in such form, as *to them* shall seem most likely to effect *their* Safety and Happiness.[4]

---

[3] Karl Barth, *The Epistle to the Romans*, 6th ed., trans. Edwyn C. Hoskyns (London, Oxford, New York: Oxford University Press, 1933 [German original: 1921; translation from the sixth edition, 1928]), pp. 27–28.

[4] John Grafton, ed., *Declaration of Independence and Other Documents of American History: 1775–1865* (New York: Dover, 2000), pp. 6–7; my emphases.

Now while St. Paul is clearly speaking of a personal authority that came to him by virtue of a direct revelation vouchsafed to him by the Lord, and while the Declaration of Independence is referring only at that point in our national history to political and governmental authority, the contrast between the two rhetorical styles (indicating therefore two quite different approaches to the sources of authority) is so different that it goes far to explain why the Catholic Church took so hostile a stance toward democracy in Europe in the nineteenth century and why the Church was so suspect here when Catholic immigrants first began to cross the Atlantic Ocean, like the Egyptians crossing the Red Sea after the Israelites into the Protestant Promised Land. Part of the reason for the hostility was the papacy's experience of the French Revolution, which largely drew an antiecclesial and anticlerical conclusion from the American rejection of monarchy. Only with the twentieth century, only with the Second Vatican Council truly, did the Church come to affirm—in a modified form, to be sure, but nonetheless truly affirm—the validity of the American view in the political sphere.

Perhaps the most succinct entry into the topic of continuity and change for my purpose comes from the address given by Pope Benedict XVI to the Cardinals of the Roman Curia on December 22, 2005, barely seven months after his election to the papacy. This address inspired the book that Prof. Matthew Levering and Fr. Matthew Lamb edited and for which I had the privilege of contributing a chapter on the conciliar document on the missionary endeavors of the Church. It is the only book I know of that has tried to respond to the Pope's methodological challenge. This point about Vatican II's reevaluation of the Church's relationship to the modern world, along with an increased appreciation of the American experiment, became the main example of the assessment of exactly what was new, and therefore discontinuous, in Vatican II, and what was part of the tradition it continued and how it did so.

What is most fascinating about this address is that Pope Benedict did not contrast the hermeneutics of discontinuity with that of *continuity*; rather, he spoke of discontinuity being bad when it leads to *rupture*; and he contrasted rupture with a hermeneutic not of continuity but of *reform*. Reform includes continuity, but it also places change as *renewal* in continuity. Here are the Pope's words:

> The question arises: Why has the implementation of the Council, in large parts of the Church, thus far been so difficult? Well, it all depends on the correct interpretation of the Council or—or we would say today—on its proper hermeneutics, the correct key to its interpretation

> and application. The problems in its implementation arose from the fact that two contrary hermeneutics came face-to-face and quarreled with each other. One caused confusion, the other, silently but more and more visibly, bore and is bearing fruit. On the one hand, there is an interpretation that I would call "a hermeneutic of discontinuity *and rupture*"; it has frequently availed itself of the sympathies of the mass media, and also one trend of modern theology. On the other, there is the "hermeneutic of *reform*," of *renewal in the continuity* of the one subject-Church, which the Lord has given to us. She is a subject that increases in time and develops, yet always remaining the same, the one subject of the journeying People of God.[5]

The trouble with taking the phrase "hermeneutic[s] of continuity" as a catchword, either of Benedict's papacy or as the lens by which one exclusively interprets Vatican II, is that it cannot, at least alone, determine what counts as continuous or discontinuous in renewal. After all, *any* change must involve *some* discontinuity, or it wouldn't be called *change*, which by definition involves some difference over time of the identity in question. Of course, if the change were so discontinuous as to result in a different identity of the thing involved in the change, then we would not speak of any continuity at all, like Cinderella's carriage reverting back to a pumpkin. This is what St. Thomas Aquinas, relying on Aristotle, calls *substantial* change. The change at the Second Vatican Council was not a substantial change of the Church.

Obviously, no council of the Church could intend that kind of change, for the Church must always remain the *Church*, what Benedict refers to as the "one subject-Church, which the Lord has given to us." For that reason, Pope Benedict speaks of the *hermeneutics of reform*, which he defines as *renewal* in continuity. In other words, as the living Body of Christ, the Church has a certain *vitality*, so that *her* continuity must be a *living* continuity, which always means both reform and renewal.

In that light, I think we can see how the extreme left and the extreme right in the Catholic Church may be judged equally (though differently) faulty. The one side captures the "rupture" represented, they claim, by the Council; the other sees the same discontinuity and rupture at work, laments and deplores it, and wants only, again they claim, continuity with the past, usually understood as a return to earlier papal condemnations of

[5] Address of His Holiness Benedict XVI to the Roman Curia, Offering Them His Christmas Greetings, Thursday, December 22, 2005; published as "Interpreting Vatican II," in *Origins* 35, no. 32 (January 26, 2006): 534–39; here, p. 536; all emphases throughout this address have been added. This address is also available in *Vatican II: Renewal within Tradition*, cited in note 1 above.

democracy, freedom of the press, separation of throne and altar, all of which were enshrined in Pope Pius IX's *Syllabus errorum.* But then, as Benedict stressed, and at first only gradually, the ground began to shift; the Church was confronted with a new situation, which demanded a different response. I will now quote the Pope directly:

> In the 19th century under Pius IX, the clash between the Church's faith and a radical liberalism and the natural sciences, which also claimed to embrace with their knowledge the whole of reality to its (knowable) limit, stubbornly proposing to make the "hypothesis of God" superfluous, had elicited from the Church a bitter and radical condemnation of this spirit of the modern age. Thus, it seemed that there was no longer any milieu open to a positive and fruitful understanding, and the rejection by those who felt they were the representatives of the modern era was also [commensurately] drastic.
>
> In the meantime, however, the modern age had also experienced developments. People came to realize that *the American Revolution* was offering a model of a modern State that differed from the theoretical model with radical tendencies that had emerged during the second phase of the French Revolution. The natural sciences were beginning to reflect more and more clearly their own limitations imposed by their own method, which, despite achieving great things, was nevertheless unable to grasp the global nature of reality. So it was that both parties were gradually beginning to open up to each other. In the period between the two World Wars and especially after the Second World War, Catholic statesmen demonstrated that a modern secular State could exist that was not neutral regarding values but alive, drawing from the great ethical sources opened by Christianity.[6]

According to Pope Benedict, only the changed circumstances outlined above can account for what was new (and therefore discontinuous *in some sense* with the past) in Vatican II, together with what it proclaimed in continuity with the past. In that regard, he holds that the Council achieved three main goals in the Church's relationship with the world. I quote him directly so you can see the subtlety of his analysis:

> It might be said that three circles of questions had formed which then, at the time of the Second Vatican Council, were expecting an answer.
>
> First of all, the relationship between faith and modern science had to be redefined. Furthermore, this did not only concern the natural sciences but also historical science. . . .

[6] Ibid., p. 537.

> Second, it was necessary to give a *new* definition to the relationship between the Church and the modern State that would make room impartially for citizens of various religions and ideologies, merely assuming responsibility for an orderly and tolerant coexistence among them and for the freedom to practice their own religion.
>
> Third, linked more generally to this was the problem of religious tolerance—a question that required a new definition of the relationship between the Christian faith and the world religions. In particular, before the recent crimes of the Nazi regime and, in general, with a retrospective look at a long and difficult history, it was necessary to evaluate and define in a new way the relationship between the Church and the faith of Israel.[7]

Now obviously, if the Council were to address these new questions and give adequate answers to them, *some* sort of discontinuity had to be involved, some development of Church teaching in these new documents insofar as the questions are different from prior ones; and the Pope is not shy at all in admitting such development. Again, he says:

> It is clear that in all these sectors, which all together form a single problem, some kind of discontinuity might emerge. Indeed, a discontinuity *had* been revealed, but in which, after the various distinctions between concrete historical situations and their requirements had been made, the continuity of principles proved not to have been abandoned. It is easy to miss this fact at a first glance.[8]

This means simply that you have to think of the level of principle, which is not easy because the media generally think only at the level of politics and personalities. To move people beyond that popular culture into an understanding of principle is challenging. However difficult, it has always been for the Church to discern, in her pilgrimage through history, where her true identity lies amidst her institutional incarnation in a world of other institutions. Nonetheless the task is hers to perform, always keeping in mind that change is undertaken, not for its own sake, but for the sake of making her evermore conformed to the will of her Lord. That is why Pope Benedict speaks not of the hermeneutics of continuity but of the hermeneutics of reform, renewal in continuity. To return to his own words once more: "*It is precisely in this combination of continuity and discontinuity at different levels that the very nature of true reform consists.*"[9]

---

[7] Ibid., pp. 537–38.

[8] Ibid., p. 538.

[9] Ibid.; emphasis added.

I think it can be regarded as more than obvious that, if Catholics could take these words to heart, the neuralgia and heat in the incessant debate between liberals and conservatives (which are political terms) would find a way toward resolution. What must be sought, continually, is the perduring identity of the Church through history *as her Lord intends her to be.* As the Pope boldly says: "The Second Vatican Council, with its new definition of the relationship between the faith of the Church and certain essential elements of modern thought, has reviewed or *even corrected* certain historical decisions, *but in this apparent discontinuity it has actually preserved and deepened her inmost nature and true identity.*"[10]

Of course, the Pope is not naïve about the nature of the world. He is, after all, the man who warned of a "dictatorship of relativism" on the eve of his election to the papacy! One *essential* part of the Church's identity is that her very presence in the world will provoke opposition. This feature of the Church formed the conclusion to Pope Benedict's 2005 Christmas address to the Roman Curia:

> The Church, both before and after the Council, was and is the same Church, one, holy, catholic and apostolic, journeying on through time; she continues "her pilgrimage amid the persecutions of the world and the consolations of God", proclaiming the death of the Lord until he comes (in glory) (cf. *Lumen Gentium* §8).
>
> Those who expected that with this fundamental "yes" to the modern era all tensions would be dispelled and that the "openness towards the world" accordingly achieved would transform everything into pure harmony, had underestimated the inner tensions as well as the contradictions inherent in the modern epoch (like every epoch).
>
> They had underestimated the perilous frailty of human nature, which has been a threat to human progress in all the periods of history and in every historical constellation. These dangers, with the new possibilities and new power of man over matter and over himself, did not disappear but instead acquired new dimensions: a look at the history of the present day shows this clearly.
>
> In our time too, the Church remains a "sign that will be opposed" (Luke 2:34)—not without reason did Pope John Paul II, then still a Cardinal, give this title to the theme for the Spiritual Exercises he preached in 1976 to Pope Paul VI and the Roman Curia. The Council could not have intended to abolish the Gospel's opposition to human dangers and errors.

---

10 Ibid.; emphasis added.

> On the contrary, it was certainly the Council's intention to overcome erroneous or superfluous contradictions in order to present to our world the requirement of the Gospel in its full greatness and purity.[11]

Hans Urs von Balthasar in his book *The God Question and Modern Man* says:

> Mankind only becomes conscious of its unity when it breaks loose from, and protests against, the claims of the Church to be the religious form of unity willed by God. This protest is wider than Protestantism in the narrow sense, but gives it some affinity with other religions of the world, and so is bound to lead to a kind of *entente cordiale* between all non-Catholic forms of religion. "Anything but this" is the common watchword by which all non-Catholics easily understand each other. In this understanding all absolute factors are gradually leveled down. . . . Hence the religion of humanitarianism can ultimately be no better recommended and demonstrated in its inner spirit than by contrasting it with Catholicism. There is no slogan nearly so suitable for summing up all the forms of cultural propaganda these days as that which promises to lead men from Catholic "narrowness" into the "breadth" of natural religion. The worldwide unity of the religions is being hammered out on the anvil of Catholicism.[12]

One of the major reasons the Second Vatican Council did not bear the fruit expected of it is because so many Catholics lost their sense of the difference between the Church and the world, their sense of their own sin and of the Church's identity as the defender of God's ultimate revelation in Christ Jesus. If Jesus can say, "They hated me without cause" (John 15:25), so must the Church say, "They hated me without cause." But Jesus also loved those who hated him and died to save them, and so must the Church love those who hate her.

How does this dynamic relate now to our own society, to American culture? If Vatican II owes so much of its teaching on the relationship between Church and world to the Church's gradual realization that the American Revolution differs in fundamental respects from the French Revolution, we must still ask, what are the uniquely American forms of the world's opposition to the Gospel? Precisely as Americans, we are of this world; we are not the kingdom of God. Here I would like to draw on an important distinction that Avery Cardinal Dulles once made in a controversial article he published in 1998 in *America* magazine called "Ortho-

---

[11] Ibid., pp. 538–39.

[12] Hans Urs von Balthasar, *The God Problem and Modern Man*, trans. Hilda Graef (New York: Seabury Press, 1967), pp. 88–89.

doxy and Social Change." According to this great American theologian, we must distinguish between political secularization recognized as good after the Second Vatican Council, versus cultural secularization, the first being (on the whole) beneficial, and the second being (again on the whole) fraught with dangers for the Church.

"In the political sense," says Cardinal Dulles, secularization "means recognition of the state as a purely secular entity. The disestablishment of religion in the American system involves obvious problems, but on the whole it has worked out well both for religion and for secular society."[13] But cultural secularization entails something much more insidious:

> In the modern situation religion tends to become marginalized, some would say trivialized. It has a very hard time maintaining itself in the public square or the market place. Any effort by a church to say what is morally permitted, required or prohibited by the law of God in the spheres of politics, medicine, business or family life is resented as an intrusion into alien territory. It is considered improper for any private association to impose its morality on people who do not belong to it. Thus religion is progressively excluded from areas in which it formerly played a decisive role. It has difficulty keeping a significant presence in education. Even in domestic life, religion plays a diminished part. As all these spheres become progressively secularized, religion retreats into its own corner. It survives as something one might decide to do with one's leisure time—almost as a hobby for people who want to be religious. Anyone who sees religion as determinative for secular activities is likely to be regarded as a fanatic. Teachers, businessmen, politicians or judges who let religion impinge in a major way on their professional activities are considered eccentric.[14]

---

[13] Avery Cardinal Dulles, S.J., "Orthodoxy and Social Change," *America* 178, no. 21 (June 20–27, 1998): 8–17; here p. 8.

[14] Ibid., p. 10. Charles Taylor seconds these observations: "[M]odern liberal political culture is characterized by an affirmation of universal human rights—to life, freedom, citizenship, self-realization—which are seen as radically unconditional; that is, they are not dependent on such things as gender, cultural belonging, civilizational development, or religious allegiance, which always limited them in the past. As long as we were living within the terms of Christendom—that is, of a civilization where the structures, institutions, and culture were all supposed to reflect the Christian nature of the society (even in the nondenominational form in which this was understood in the early United States)—we could never have attained this radical unconditionality" (Charles Taylor, "A Catholic Modernity?" in *A Catholic Modernity: Charles Taylor's Marianist Award Lecture*, ed. James L. Heft, S.M. [New York: Oxford University Press, 1999], pp. 16–17).

These insights are hardly new, but the key point is that they lead inexorably to the conclusion, by Dulles again: "If the social analysis in the opening section of this article is correct, it should be evident that to be orthodox in our society it is necessary to be countercultural."[15] What happened to American Catholicism after the Council can be summed up by saying that too many Catholics embraced the modern world, the liberal, secularized cultural polity of our time, not all wrong but nonetheless dangerous, without taking into account how the Church in *any* age must be in some tension with the culture of the time. That was why I said, in what counts as one of my more controversial statements, that "liberal Catholicism is an exhausted project."[16] That statement has come back to haunt me again and again, but what I meant must be understood in the context of what I have said here.

I would criticize some versions also of conservative Catholicism for claiming the mantle of a hermeneutic of simple continuity without giving due allowance for what Pope Benedict means by a hermeneutic of reform, which must entail at least some aspects of discontinuity. Let me mention two instances of the kind of tension that has been reduced by grabbing one horn and forgetting the other. The first is the Lefebvrist attempt to say that Catholicism cannot change in any manner, lest it betray its identity. The Society of St. Pius X's opposition to Vatican II has threatened Church unity, but similar threats following a council are nothing new in Church history. The most recent previous example was the "Old Catholics," who rejected the First Vatican Council's definitions of papal primacy and infallibility as betrayals of Catholic tradition and Catholic identity. The Society of St. Pius X charges Vatican II with similar betrayals.

The fundamental theological question is this: Can there be a development of Catholic traditions, which is not a betrayal but a sign of vitality? The Lefebvrist movement was not primarily liturgical in its conception. Some of it was fueled by liturgical nostalgia or by the authentic conviction that liturgy is truly worship of God and not a community meal. That is true, but that is not what Lefebvre worried about. Lefebvre was a very intelligent man who knew that the conciliar decrees' proclamation of religious freedom, the teaching about the Church, the priesthood of all believers based in baptism, and ecumenical and interfaith dialogue, were, from his perspective, unilateral departure from revealed truth; they were a rupture.

---

[15] Dulles, "Orthodoxy," p. 10.

[16] I made this remark more or less extempore in an unrehearsed homily at a Mass for a meeting of the National Center for the Laity in Chicago on January 17, 1998, and then expanded it into an article for *Commonweal* which has been republished in my aforementioned book, *The Difference God Makes*, pp. 155–72.

On the other side, we have those who would also argue that Vatican II was indeed a rupture with Catholic tradition—necessary so that the Church could catch up with modernity and conform to American culture. This group resurrects arguments made by Paul Blanchard a generation ago. Paul Blanchard's book *American Freedom and Catholic Power* was on the *New York Times*' best-seller list in 1949 and 1950 for eleven months. It claimed that the Catholic problem was still with us in America and called for the formation of a resistance movement to Catholicism. Decades later, Blanchard's bigotry is no longer directly defended in educated circles. Questions remain, though, concerning why Blanchard's ideas made progress in some of the most important and intelligent American academic and political circles throughout much of the culture of the day. Was Blanchard onto something necessarily subversive about Catholics? In my generation, I'd have wanted to say no. But we should look at it again. Are Catholics' commitments not compatible with the demands of American democratic philosophy and practice, at least in some sense? Where lies the discontinuity between Catholic faith and American culture?

Today some scholars try to solve the Blanchard problem by changing the topic, which connects questions of ecclesial authority and the faithful's relationship to it. They argue, "Ours is now a liberal Catholicism, and therefore the problem posed by the unmodified Catholicism that Blanchard targeted more than half a century ago doesn't really exist." We have accommodated ourselves as believers to a popular liberal culture. The United States is a classically liberal country. We have no landed gentry. We are a people of choice, and enculturation of the faith in our context means liberalizing our religion.

If, however, we refuse to change the topic on the ground that the Catholic Church has not changed substantially, the problem of authoritative teaching remains. As Pope John Paul II noted in 1991, all those who are "convinced that they know the truth, and firmly adhere to it, are considered unreliable from a democratic point of view."[17] Perhaps, therefore, Blanchard was right in worrying that Catholics had principled reservations about the scope of democratic legitimacy and the sweep of democratic authority. It is widely and justly celebrated that the Second Vatican Council declared the natural human right to liberty of conscience, but what the same council said about the liberty of the Church is little noticed. And yet that is where the tensions are today. While one might have an individual right to express whatever religious oddities one wishes, Americans admit, that is not to permit the Church to have an institutional right that allows

[17] John Paul II, *Centesimus Annus* (May 1, 1991), ch. 5, no. 46.

her to be a player in the shaping of society. The Vatican Council's decree on religious liberty was, however, as strong on the liberty of the Church as it was on the liberty of individual human conscience. Little noticed, but also significant, is that the same council said nothing directly about the institution of democracy. In light of that and other facts, faithful Catholics might be considered unreliable from a "democratic" point of view to the extent that they, in and through the Church, insist that the democratic social and political order must be conformed to higher law through means that are both rooted in and conform to valid positive law based upon natural human morality, natural law.

What can we say in conclusion? What American Catholics must first do is to answer this question, first for themselves and then to their neighbors, whatever their political persuasions might be here or in any particular polity or culture on the face of the earth: Why be orthodox? Here is Father Dulles's answer:

> In their hearts people long for something more than what is offered by the secular order, with its passing pleasures and fluctuating opinions. They reach out for something higher, something universally and eternally good and true, to which they can give themselves permanently and totally. This is precisely what revealed religion has to offer. It tells us that God, the uncreated source of all truth and goodness, has freely communicated himself and his divine life by bestowing himself in his divine Son and his Holy Spirit. God has established in Christ a sacred order, a way of salvation. The church, founded upon Christ, and secondarily upon Peter and the Apostles, has been established in the world to give permanent testimony to the saving truth and to nourish the faithful with holy rites that put them in contact with the saving realities. The church has been equipped by God with hierarchical structures to preserve its apostolic heritage to prevent it from succumbing to the shifting tides of popular opinion. Faith, as a way to salvation, involves submission to the authoritative teaching that comes from God through the church. Faith therefore cherishes orthodoxy.[18]

That last sentence, I think, summarizes the fundamental challenge of Catholicism to American culture today. It explains why there must never be rupture and always be continuity in change. Only if Catholics truly and deeply *cherish* orthodoxy—that is, the very truth that comes from God—can the Church be of real service to American culture. If the pursuit of happiness is central to the American project, which it is, we

---

[18] Dulles, "Orthodoxy," p. 14.

Catholics need to be confident that we can freely show our fellow citizens the way to that happiness by our witness and by our persuasiveness.

While Vatican II changed how the Church views political secularization or this worldly reality, the essentially otherworldly hope that is intrinsic to her Gospel message—the preservation of which is the essence of orthodoxy—will always keep the Church in tension and partially at odds with any purely political and social constructs, democratic or otherwise, in every age.

CHAPTER 2

The Millennial Challenge of Catholicism in America

FR. MATTHEW L. LAMB
Ave Maria University

THE CULTIVATION of intelligence is a cooperative enterprise down the ages. The languages, words, sciences, theories, arts—all we learn from others. There is no Robinson Crusoe or Cartesian universal doubter in the realms of reason. As Cardinal Newman astutely observed traditions are crucial, not just for believers, but for all human learners. Belief and knowledge processing down the ages are symbiotically cooperative in the realms of mind, heart, and imagination. We could imagine it as a long, multimillennial procession of teachers and learners down the generations. I shall sketch some developments that have been largely ignored in American culture. The recovery of these developments is most important if America is to meet the internal and global issues facing the country in the twenty-first century.

Pope John Paul II emphasized the importance of a "free search for the whole truth about nature, man and God." He continued:

> The present age is in urgent need of . . . disinterested service, namely of *proclaiming the meaning of truth*, that fundamental good without which freedom, justice, and human dignity are extinguished. By means of a kind of universal humanism a Catholic University is completely dedicated to the research of all aspects of truth in their essential connection with the supreme Truth, who is God. It does this without fear but rather with enthusiasm, dedicating itself to every path of knowledge, aware of being preceded by him who is "the Way, the Truth, and the Life", the Logos, whose Spirit of intelligence and love enables the human person with his or her own intelligence to find the ultimate reality of which He is the source and end and who

> alone is capable of giving fully that Wisdom without which the future of the world would be in danger.[1]

The responsibility to explore "the whole truth about nature, man and God" means that today there is a need to articulate the challenge measuring up to the achievements of the past. The contributors to this book make reference to cultural influences that have resulted from the progenitors of modern cultures who did not measure up to past achievements. References are made to nominalism and voluntarism as eclipsing the practice of reason guiding will, resulting in failures that endanger the future of the world. Differing practices of reason were developed in the first and second millennia. Ways of integrating these different practices is the challenge of the third millennium.

First Millennium and the Intellectual Tradition

During the first millennium of Christianity the task of nurturing learning and intelligence found a stable home or institution in the thousands of monasteries and cathedral schools where hundreds of thousands of men and women kept alive the sacred words of Scripture, the writings of the Fathers of the Church, as well as the classic literature of East and West. Teaching, learning, and the intellectual life were practiced within the orientations of the monks, nuns, clerics, and lay students toward wisdom and holiness. The Greek and Latin Fathers were able to incorporate the best of their philosophical sources into a Christian Hellenism that preserved both reason and the Christian faith.[2] St. Justin, philosopher and martyr, saw the "seeds of the Logos sown among all men of all times so that those who lived virtuously, like Socrates, were of Christ."[3] St. Clement of Alexandria centers his *Stromata* around the Logos as creator of the universe and manifested in the Law of the Old Testament, the philosophy of the Greeks, and, finally, most perfectly in Jesus Christ, who is the Word of God Incarnate. Following Irenaeus, Hippolytus of Rome's valuable *Philosophumena* argues that "the opinions advanced by the philosophers of the Greeks . . .

---

[1] Pope John Paul II, Apostolic Constitution *Ex Corde Ecclesiae* [From the Heart of the Church] (August 15, 1990), 4; emphasis in original.

[2] See Pope Benedict XVI, "Faith, Reason and the University: Memories and Reflections" (lecture, University of Regensburg, Germany, September 12, 2006): "A profound encounter of faith and reason is taking place here, an encounter between genuine enlightenment and religion. From the very heart of Christian faith and, at the same time, the heart of Greek thought now joined to faith, . . . [so that] [n]ot to act 'with *logos*' is contrary to God's nature," sec. 24.

[3] Justin, *Apologia* 1.46, 2.10.

are of greater antiquity than those [heresies], and more deserving of reverence in reference to their views respecting the divinity."[4]

Even Tertullian with his antipathy to pagan philosophy—he posed the question: What has Athens to do with Jerusalem, the academy with the Church?—acknowledged his debt to Seneca and drew on the Stoics. St. Augustine emphasizes the importance of Cicero and the Platonists in his arduous intellectual conversion narrated in books 5 through 7 of his *Confessions*. St. Augustine is a good guide to such an intellectual life, steeped as he was in the great Latin classics of his day.

The salvation of intelligence and desire or will is fundamental in Augustine's religious conversion. Far from blinding his mind and heart, faith in Jesus Christ assisted Augustine in discovering the higher, more sublime dimensions of his mind, for our hearts are restless till they rest in God. The theological is the salvation of the theoretic-contemplative and the practical-political ways of life. From the great Greek and Roman philosophers, Augustine glimpsed the importance of striving for wisdom, attuning his mind and heart to the whole of reality and ordering his appetites and emotions intelligently toward the truly good. Yet he also saw how these philosophers were unable to give adequate accounts for why so few—and Augustine knew he had not—attained the life of speculative wisdom. Moreover, they could not account for evil and injustice to Augustine's satisfaction. The philosophical agnosticism stated by Socrates at the end of the *Apology*, "I go to die, you to live; but which of us goes to a better reality is unknown to all but God," was no match for the disorder and evil of human history and of Augustine's own wayward living.

Fundamental to Augustine's conversion is his discovery of an ordered practice of intelligence and reason. The intellectual aspects of Augustine's conversion are especially present in books 5 through 9 of his *Confessions*. His ascent to God was accompanied by an awareness of the importance, not only of understanding (*intellectus*), but also of judging that the understanding is true—of Veritas. For Augustine, the nature of the human mind is given and to be discovered—it is not self-constructed, as for many moderns.[5] Augustine narrates his conversion to Christ as integral to his quest for intellectual and moral excellence. Truth is divine, and truth beckons intelligence to a love and understanding that both confirms and elevates human knowing and loving. So, at the beginning of book 7 of the *Confessions*, Augustine mentions how he was so "gross of mind" (*incrassatus corde*) that he had not come to the

[4] Hippolytus, *Philosophumena*, bk. 1, Prooemium (Prologue).

[5] See Ernest L. Fortin, *The Birth of Philosophic Christianity: Studies in Early Christian and Medieval Thought*, ed. J. Brian Benestad (Lanham, Md.: Rowman and Littlefield, 1996), pp. 10–11, 21–122.

realization of how the mind, while it generates all images, is not itself an image "but altogether different than such images."[6] Augustine uses "*cor*," or heart, to designate the mind with its orienting desire or will.[7] Here, of course, he is echoing Matthew 13:15 to indicate how his own attentive consciousness (*intentionem*) has been so dulled by his disordered desires and sinful living that he cannot grasp that the mind both forms all images and transcends them.[8] This twofold aspect of mind, both forming all images and yet not being itself a material image, is developed in his *De trinitate*, where Augustine explores the human mind as an immaterial "*imago Dei.*"[9]

In his *Confessions*, Augustine reflects on the nature of human intelligence as it judges something to be true and another thing false: "So, as I reflected on how it was that I came to make these judgments which I did make, I discovered above my changing mind an unchanging and true eternity of truth."[10] He then recounts how he ascended from sensible and corporeal things to the faculty of reason and the intelligible and intelligent light by which he is led to prefer the true and eternal to the changeable. The realism of this presencing of eternal truth is clear when Augustine narrates that this intellectual conversion to truth is a discovery of Being: "And in the flash of a trembling glance my mind came to That Which Is. I understood the invisible through those things that were created."[11] But he immediately adds that this discovery was not yet habitual. For he could not live the theoretic or contemplative life demanded by the discovery until Christ gave him the strength to do so.[12]

---

[6] St. Augustine, *Confessions* 7.1.

[7] See Edgardo de la Peza, *El significado de "cor" en San Agustín* (Paris, 1962).

[8] Matthew 13:15: "For this people's heart has grown dull, and their ears are heavy of hearing, and their eyes they have closed, lest they should perceive with their eyes, and hear with their ears, and understand with their heart, and turn for me to heal them."

[9] See D. J. Merriell, *To the Image of the Trinity: A Study in the Development of Aquinas' Teaching* (Toronto: Pontifical Institute of Medieval Studies, 1990), pp. 13–35, 98–110, on Augustine. Also John M. Rist, *Augustine: Ancient Thought Baptized* (Cambridge, UK: Cambridge University Press, 1996), pp. 92–147, on Augustine's non-Platonic understanding of body, soul, and mind.

[10] *Confessions* 7.17; in Latin: "hoc ergo quaerens, unde iudicarem, cum ita iudicarem, inueneram inconmutabilem et ueram uertitatis aeternitatem supra mentem meam conmutabilem."

[11] Ibid.: "et peruenit ad id, quod est in ictu trepidantis aspectus. tunc uero inuisibilia tua per ea quae facta sunt intellecta conspexi."

[12] See the end of *Confessions* 8, where Augustine converts to Christ. That conversion enables him to live morally and intellectually. This is a classic expression of the ascent to truth as God that Augustine shares with his mother, illustrating how the light of faith enables souls to enjoy a contemplation of the Divine, even if they lack formal intellectual training (see *Confessions* 9.10).

To understand eternity required both an appropriation of intelligence as not intrinsically conditioned by space or time, and a grasp of the concreteness of being known by judgment.[13] Both elements are in the narratives of Augustine's ascent to the intelligible and "That Which Is" (*ad id quod est*). The spiritual nature of intelligence together with the Veritas of true judgment is the ground for understanding God as the eternal creating and redeeming the temporal. Truth's transcendence of space and time does not negate space and time, but rather affirms it. The contrast with Plotinus could not be more graphically illustrated than in the two passages in the *Confessions* in which Augustine narrates an ascent to the eternal God. In both places, at the very apogee of his mind's union with the Divine, Augustine writes of "visible things," "fragrance," and the wealth of an eternal wisdom "where You feed Israel forever with the food of truth."[14]

There are two aspects of intellectual conversion in Augustine. One is the conversion away from materialism that limited reality to bodies. In this respect intellectual conversion can proceed among the Platonists. The second aspect is conversion *toward* the created material world. Here there is a

---

13 See *Confessions* 7.17: "I was altogether certain that Your *invisible things are clearly seen from the creation of the world, being understood by the things that are made*: so too are Your everlasting power and Your Godhead. I was now studying the ground of my admiration for the beauty of bodies, whether celestial or of earth, and on what authority I might rightly judge of things mutable and say, "This ought to be so, that not so." Enquiring then what was the source of my judgment, when I did so judge I had discovered the immutable and true eternity of truth above my changing mind. Thus by stages I passed from bodies to the soul which uses the body for its perceiving, and from this to the soul's inner power, to which the body's senses present external things, as indeed the beasts are able; and from there I passed on to the reasoning power, to which is referred for judgment what is received from the body's senses. This too realised that it was mutable in me, and rose to its own understanding. It withdrew my thought from its habitual way, abstracting from the confused crowds of phantasms that it might find what light suffused it, when with utter certainty it cried aloud that the immutable was to be preferred to the mutable, and how it had come to know the immutable itself: for if it had not come to some knowledge of the immutable, it could not have known it as certainly preferable to the mutable. Thus in the thrust of a trembling glance (see I Cor. 15:52) my mind arrived at That Which Is. (see Exodus 3:14) Then indeed I saw clearly Your *invisible things which are understood by the things that are made* (see Rom. 1:20); but I lacked the strength to hold my gaze fixed, and my weakness was beaten back again so that I returned to my old habits, bearing nothing with me but a memory of delight and a desire as for something of which I had caught the fragrance but which I had not yet the strength to eat." This translation is from Augustine's *Confessions* by F. J. Sheed, second edition by Michael P. Foley (Indianapolis, Ind.: Hackett, 2006), pp. 132–33.

14 See *Confessions* 7.17, 9.10.

profound difference between the Platonists and Augustine. The Platonists were unable to turn toward the true God who enlightens every human being who comes into the world. They could only turn toward their own minds and toward a god, as with Plotinus, who was so utterly transcendent to the world that that god was *contrary* to the material world. Augustine sees how that is a position of pride, a failure to accept all of creation as good. So Augustine ends book 7 with a turn first to Christ as the mediator between God and man, and then to Paul. The contradictions between the law of "my members" and "the law of my mind" (see Romans 7:23) showed Augustine how, in order for intellectual conversion to be toward the truth of the Word Incarnate, it had to be accompanied by moral conversion.[15] As Fortin remarks, the difference between Augustine and many present-day thinkers lies in the fact "that Augustine was intent on preserving and restoring human wholeness by directing all of the individual's activities to the goal or goals to which they are intrinsically ordered."[16]

In Jesus Christ, God has made known to us how death and evil are overcome. Reason is enlightened and strengthened by faith toward a full understanding and knowledge in God. Without the light of faith, the heart of reason is darkened by the shadows of widespread evil and injustice. With the other Fathers of the Church Augustine showed that without the light of faith the intellectually excellent or virtuous were led by all the evil and malice in human history to resort to a cynicism stifling the love of wisdom and truth. Every page of human history is bloodied by countless acts of violence and injustice. Without the light of faith, the morally excellent or virtuous slide into either a stoic withdrawal from the suffering of others or into an epicurean distraction from the pain of the world. So his conversion to Christ, his graced realization that Jesus Christ is risen and is indeed the Word Incarnate who founded and by his Spirit guides "our mother the Catholic Church," actually enabled Augustine to cultivate the intellectual and moral virtues that previously had eluded him. Jesus reveals to us the kingdom of God in eternal life, and so we can in the face of all the evil and injustice of this world continue to strive for the wholeness of truth and the justice of the good life.

Living a disordered and sinful life blinds one to the higher aspects of one's reason, to the wisdom needed to order one's senses, imagination, and

---

15 Some, including E. Gilson, tend to misread Augustine's intellectual conversion as a dichotomy between sensation and intelligence in line with a Cartesian dualism of mind and body. While this might be true of some later so-called Augustinians, it is not the case with Augustine himself. On the consonance of Augustine with Aquinas's realism, see references in Merriel's book in footnote 9 above.

16 Fortin, *Birth of Philosophic Christianity*, p. 10.

actions toward the truly good. Unlike Greek and Latin philosophers, Augustine affirmed how the whole of material creation is iconic of Divine Beauty. Like an icon, the whole created universe is suffused by the light of the Triune God's glory when the rational soul is ordered to be truly good. Augustine could fully appropriate the classical importance of the intellectual and moral virtues only in the context of his own religious conversion to Jesus Christ with the attendant theological virtues of faith, hope, and charity. All sin is basically a depersonalization of created goods, violently tearing them from the good and beautiful order in which God creates and sustains them. This privation of the good order, this depersonalization, Augustine dramatizes in the first four books of his *Confessions*, where he gives no personal names of his friends or that of his mistress. For he realized that he was not loving them for who they were in God, but that he was abusing them to satisfy his own disordered desires.

What is more, all the violence in the world is rooted in the violent and prideful refusal of God's loving presence. His *City of God* lays out the horror of the constant wars fueled by the "libido dominandi"—the disordered desire for domination. Hell is everlasting warfare and violence rooted in pride and arrogant disordered love of one's own idolatrous glory. In his *The Literal Meaning of Genesis*, Augustine articulates the two contradictory and opposed loves.[17]

From the fall of the evil angels to the massive totalitarianisms and tyrannies of our times, disordered love seeks to depersonalize and destroy the beauty of God's creation. But Jesus Christ has risen. We must keep the eyes of our heart on the communion of saints, where we shall come into the new heavens and the new earth. Christ's revelation of eternal life enables Augustine to dedicate himself to the good life of the intellectual and moral virtues. What we do in this life affects how we shall be for all eternity. Death and injustice do not have the last word—the Word Incarnate risen from the dead does.[18]

---

[17] See St. Augustine, *The Literal Meaning of Genesis*: "[O]ne love is holy, the other disordered; one turned towards the neighbor, the other fixated on self; one looking to the common good, keeping in view the society of saints in heaven, the other trying to force the common good under its own power, arrogantly looking to domination; one subject to God, the other rivaling Him; one tranquil, the other tempestuous; one peaceful, the other seditious; one preferring truth to false praise, the other eager for praise of any sort; one friendly, the other envious; one wishing for its neighbor what it wishes for itself, the other seeking to subject its neighbor to itself; one looking for its neighbor's advantage, the other looking only for its own advantage" (New York: Newman Press, 1982), trans. John Taylor, vol. II, pp. 147–48.

[18] See St. Augustine, *Against the Academicians*, trans. Peter King (Indianapolis, Ind.: Hackett, 1995).

St. Augustine and countless other men and women in the first millennium manifested the many ways that a vibrant and loving faith in Christ fosters the intellectual apostolate. They evangelized Europe by uniting in their many communities worship and contemplative holiness and wisdom with the tasks of cultivating the intellectual and moral virtues, as well as all the skills, crafts, and art so manifest in the towering beauty of cathedrals. The gargoyles, however, warned of the omnipresence of evil and ignorance and disorder. In his criticisms of Abelard and the new "scientia dialectica," St. Bernard voiced his concern that the quest for science and scholarship might foster pride and all the bitter fruits of pride that brought down the classical achievements of Greece and Rome. Without wisdom and holiness, science and scholarship could sell their skills to the highest bidders who wanted to be like gods.

Second Millennium and the Intellectual Tradition

At the dawn of the second millennium the achievements of all these "scholae Domini," or schools of the Lord as cathedral schools were called, gave rise to the universities in which the intellectual tradition would be carried out under a more focused quest for science and scholarship.[19] Using the metaphor of a procession, a new direction was taken in the West. As with all things Catholic, the new did not dispense with the old. We still have the intellectual tradition carried on in monasteries, seminaries, and convents. Thanks to the new direction, the small seeds that sprung up in Catholic Europe during the "ages of faith," universities now span the globe. New forms of religious life emerged to meet this concern. The mendicant Dominicans and Franciscans, and later the Jesuits and other religious and lay organizations in the Church, took up the challenge of keeping the burgeoning sciences, humanities, and arts from being cut off from the quest for wisdom and holiness.[20]

St. Thomas Aquinas wrote: "It is actually natural to man to strive for knowledge of the truth." John Paul II writes of the perennial "novitas" of the work of Aquinas.[21] The English "originality" does not capture the meaning of "novitas" as newness, surprising unfamiliarity. The Holy Father himself experienced this startling strangeness of Aquinas's work as a

---

[19] See C. Stephen Jaeger, *Envy of Angels: Cathedral Schools and Social Ideals in Medieval Europe 950–1200* (Philadelphia: University of Pennsylvania Press, 1994).

[20] On the emergence of universities in Europe, see Hastings Rashdall, *Universities of Europe in the Middle Ages*, new ed. (New York: Oxford University Press, 1942); also Olaf Petersen, *The First Universities* (Cambridge: Cambridge University Press, 2007).

[21] See Pope John Paul II, Encyclical Letter *Fides et Ratio* (September 14, 1998), 43.

professor. His writings illustrate how Aquinas provides an explanatory framework of wisdom, both philosophical and theological, that is open to all the genuine discoveries of the sciences, all serious historical scholarship. As is clear from his synthesis of metaphysics and aspects of phenomenology, the Pope sees that Aquinas offers an approach to wisdom that heuristically attunes those studying his work to the patterns of the whole of creation and redemption.[22] Indeed, if we are to bring together the quest for wisdom and holiness with the quest for science and scholarship, the Pope stresses the foundational importance of metaphysics.[23]

Metaphysics is important, not only for serious theology, but as a foundation for the sciences, humanities, and arts, if these are to overcome fragmentation and the isolation that hinders interdisciplinary collaboration. Metaphysical wisdom provides a comprehensive heuristic framework capable of attuning the mind to the intelligibility of the whole of reality—to being as being. Aquinas clearly grasped how wisdom is both a divine gift and a natural aspiration of the human mind that sets the acquisition of speculative and practical wisdom as intellectual excellence or virtues. Divine gifts neither deny nor denigrate human abilities. For these natural capacities are themselves the gifts of God's creative love. So the theological virtues call forth and encourage the journey of acquiring the human intellectual and moral virtues.[24]

With Augustine and the Fathers, Aquinas distinguishes between the orientation of the mind toward the sensible and imaginable and the orientation of the mind to know itself, and through understanding its own spiritual nature, to reach a true analogical knowledge of angels and God.[25] By attending to his own operations of knowing and loving, Aquinas grasped the central importance of this immaterial image of God as the highest created analogue to understand the central mystery of the Triune God.

As the human mind longs for correct answers, so this desire for truth leads to wisdom. Wisdom is acquired, according to Aquinas, insofar as the

---

22 See ibid., 44.

23 Ibid., 83: "We face a great challenge at the end of this millennium to move from *phenomenon to foundation*, a step as necessary as it is urgent. We cannot stop short at experience alone; even if experience does reveal the human being's interiority and spirituality, speculative reflection must penetrate to the spiritual substance and the foundation on which it depends. Therefore, a notion of philosophy which denies any room for metaphysics would be radically unsuited to the task of mediation in the understanding of revelation" (emphasis in original).

24 See Thomas Aquinas, *Summa Theologiae* I–II, questions 55–70.

25 From Augustine, Aquinas takes the teaching on "ratio inferior" and "ratio superior"; see Robert Mulligan, S.J., "*Ratio Superior and Ratio Inferior: The Historical Background*," in *The New Scholasticism* 29, no. 1 (1955): 1–32.

human mind moves from knowing sensible objects (e.g., physics), through imaginative objects (e.g., mathematics), to attending to spiritual or immaterial realities (e.g., metaphysics of being). The higher in no way negate the lower. Metaphysics provides a wise understanding of the intelligible order in the whole range of beings, material and spiritual, as well as in the range of sciences and mathematical disciplines.[26]

To understand what Pope John Paul II in *Fides et Ratio* calls "the surprising newness" of Aquinas is to grasp how Aquinas links the way of wisdom with judgment. Thinking and concepts are not enough. We know in the act of correctly judging; and true judgments are not limited to sensible and imaginative beings. Aquinas states: "There are realities that transcend both the senses and the imagination, namely, those that are entirely independent of matter both with respect to their being (esse) and with respect to their being understood. So, when we know realities of this kind through judgment, our knowledge must terminate neither in the imagination nor in the senses."[27]

While our spiritual minds can know—not just think about—spiritual realities, our minds can also know material realities. The higher in no way negates the lower. There is here neither a Platonist nor a Cartesian opposition between the spiritual and the material, between mind (res cogitans) and bodies (res extensa). Aquinas analyzes in detail how the light of active intelligence illumines the human imagination, grasping the intelligibility in the phantasm (species qua) and understanding the universal in the particular (species quae), then intelligently formulating the universal common to many in the concept (species in qua). The intelligible is not a kind of "looking" with the senses alone; nor is it an imaginative looking at images alone. All the senses and the imagination provide the mind with givens to be understood. It is the light of active intelligence that grasps the intelligible and so the universal in the particular.[28]

There is no antinomy between the universal and the particular, no contradiction between a singular thing and the species and genus to which it belongs. Aquinas states how by that light of active intelligence we can know truly and unchangeably very changeable and contingent things and events. He states: "For the light of agent intellect is needed by which we can know unchangeable truth in changeable things, and distinguish the things themselves from the likenesses of things."[29]

---

[26] Aquinas, *In Boethius de Trinitate*, 5–6.

[27] Ibid., 6, 2c.

[28] On this see Bernard Lonergan, *Verbum: Word and Idea in Aquinas* (Toronto: University of Toronto Press, 1997), pp. 1–105.

[29] *Summa Theologiae* I, q. 84, a. 6, ad 1.

The fact is that we do know God by both reason and faith. By reason we can come to know that God exists. By faith we know that God is Father, Son, and Holy Spirit. We know all the mysteries of the divine and Catholic faith. The assent or judgment of faith, as Aquinas repeats, ends through the propositions of judgment at the realities themselves.[30] The wise act of judging, whether in metaphysics or in faith, knows the Divine Realities. We do not just know our concepts or ideas about God, as if we were locked up in a Cartesian or Kantian subjectivism—we know God! But we in no way comprehend God—comprehensibility regards the first act of the mind as understanding. Even in the beatific vision no created intelligence can comprehend the Triune God.

Third Millennium Challenge

The distinction between the sensible and intelligible is relevant today. Learning the sciences requires an intellectual asceticism, a training of the mind to move beyond the descriptive categories of sense to the explanatory categories of mathematical and scientific specializations of intelligence. It is a great irony, not lost on so illustrious a physicist as Werner Heisenberg, that the emergence of modern empirical science continued orientations of classic Platonic and Aristotelian philosophy and yet was used to displace classical philosophy and scholasticism in the academy.[31] The empirical natural sciences have transformed the world of nature and of history profoundly. The flourishing of the sciences, both natural and human, is matched by the immense labors of historical scholarship, and the brilliance of the many literary, artistic, and architectural achievements. The third millennium of Catholicism demands the development of wisdom as an understanding of the interrelations of the sciences among themselves (interdisciplinary studies as cutting edge) and with the humanities and arts.

However, as the nineteenth and twentieth centuries unfolded, humanity experienced a dark side of the radical European Enlightenment. If the second millennium began by differentiating wisdom and science, it ended with a complete loss of any notion of wisdom as a serious theoretical attunement to the whole. With the loss of wisdom traditions, modern cultures cultivated empirical sciences of the particular in ways that led to the

---

30 Ibid., II–II, q. 1, a. 2, ad 2.

31 Werner Heisenberg's father was a professor of Middle and Modern Greek; the young Werner read the dialogues of Plato and invoked Aristotle's notion of "potency" in relation to quantum indeterminacy; see Werner Heisenberg, *Physics and Philosophy* (New York: Harper Classics, 2007), pp. 15, 27, 134, 154–55.

fragmentation of culture. There is no heuristic attention to the intelligibility and pattern of the whole; instead there is attention only to the individual things, and any efforts to pattern or order them are taken to be conventional and arbitrary. Wisdom is replaced by the will to power.

Pope Benedict XVI indicated that this break with the efforts to integrate science and scholarship with wisdom and holiness began with the nominalism of Duns Scotus. Duns Scotus did not study Augustine with the depth and comprehension of Aquinas. He did not grasp *theoria* as a way of living, requiring an intellectual conversion, whereby one can understand that the intelligible causes the sensible. Several key oversights follow from this failure on the part of Scotus, oversights that would increase as his influence spread.[32] His error was deepened by Ockham and successive philosophers and theologians through the Reformation and Enlightenment. Reason was left with only sensations versus concepts, so that we only know "concepts" rather than real beings. There was a massive eclipse of judgment as knowing the real. Universals are only flatus vocis, empty words used to arbitrarily label fragmented individual entities or, in Leibniz's terms, monads.

Despite efforts to counteract it by realists, nominalism spread, replacing wisdom with increasingly fragmented attention to particulars in isolation from their natures and ends within the universe of being. Metaphysics was increasingly truncated and distorted by a conceptualism that failed to attend to (1) the objective abstraction whereby objects define sensation and intellectual light, and (2) the acts of judging as affirming or denying the composition of subject and predicate and so affirming or denying being as esse. Nominalism exalted the will over reason, breaking any living continuity with the great philosophical and theological traditions of the past. Doctrinal and theoretical traditions were devalued into purely "textual" and "verbal" matters. The challenge posed by nominalism is to overcome the dualism between mind and body, between empirical science and theoretical wisdom, that became massive in modernity and leads to contemporary relativism, historicism, and nihilism.

Benedict Spinoza's *Theological-Political Treatise* fragmented the Bible just as nature had been fragmented, so that all order is arbitrary power imposing order. Spinoza reduced the Bible into discrete sentences; there are no whole books, let alone the Bible as a whole. One text can only find meaning relative to other texts. He provided historicist-reductive founda-

---

[32] See Pope Benedict XVI, "Faith, Reason and the University" (Regensburg lecture), sec. 25; also James V. Schall, *The Regensburg Lecture* (South Bend, Ind.: St. Augustine Press, 2007), pp. 63–68; and Etienne Gilson, *The Unity of Philosophical Experience* (San Francisco: Ignatius Press, 1999), pp. 61–121.

tions to a historical-critical method that treated the Bible as any other text. As Newton's mechanics sought only three-dimensional, perceptible motions, so Spinoza's canons of interpretation recognize only those perceptible textual meanings found in the Scriptures as a perceptible book. The texts are not to be taken as true when they are referring to any realities not perceptible by the human senses. Spinoza makes clear that biblical interpretation does not concern itself with the truth of the texts but only with perceptible meanings. There can be no spiritual realities revealed in Scripture.[33]

This development has a special philosophical meaning for American culture, as the following essay by Professor Lawler will indicate. The new Enlightenment culture of the United States was particularly vulnerable to nominalism with its insistence that only isolated individual things exist and that all orders are imposed arbitrarily by will. From late-medieval nominalism through the Reformation and Romanticism, Americans, along with their modern European counterparts, sought to liberate human life and nature from Logos and what they considered the "cold constraints of reason." Science was handed over to mathematical hardheadedness, and voluntarism took over the fields of morality and religion. Hobbes and Locke did away with the Hellenic Christian cosmos of an omniscient and loving Triune God. Humans were orphaned in a cold, indifferent nature. Monads without purpose, they had to turn to what Hobbes termed the "prosthetic divinity" of their engineering and technology in the war against hostile environments and other men. The so-called wars of religion led Spinoza, Hobbes, Locke, and other political philosophers to privatize revealed religion—or to reject it outright as with Marx. Religion could no longer provide a wisdom ordering societies, while war was read into the very marrow of nature and humanity. They threw out the baby (religion) and kept the bloody bathwater of wars and violence as intrinsic to nature, both cosmic and human.

One of the greatest of American mathematicians and philosophers, Charles S. Peirce, realized the enormity of the threat posed by nominalism. He saw nominalism as pervasive throughout the modern era. Professor Paul Forster has provided a thorough analysis of Peirce's analysis and critique of nominalism.[34] Unfortunately, Peirce saw in Duns Scotus an ally for realism. He sought to disengage Scotus from Ockham's more radical nominalism. Had he studied more carefully the Augustinian and Thomist attention to the operations of knowing as fundamental to the origin of both concepts

---

33 See Spinoza, *Theological-Political Treatise*, ed. Jonathan Israel (Cambridge: Cambridge University Press, 2007), pp. 97–100.

34 Paul Forster, *Peirce and the Threat of Nominalism* (Cambridge: Cambridge University Press, 2011).

and the truth of judgments as knowing real things, he would have had a more solid realist alternative to nominalism than his pragmatism.[35] Using a metaphor from Fr. Bernard Lonergan, Peirce's pragmatism is still caught in a Scotistic conceptualism, and so is a half-way house between nominalism and a fully verifiable and verified metaphysical realism.[36]

A long procession of saints, scholars, scientists, and artists in the last two centuries of the second millennium sought to defend the dignity of human life and to overcome the fragmentation of an instrumentalist degradation of human reason. Pope Benedict XVI calls attention to the saints, martyrs, holy scholars, and artists who have keep alive the intellectual apostolate that proceeds from the heart of the Church. For the two-millennial procession of Catholicism means that its third millennium offers hope. The procession is not, despite all appearances to the contrary, doomed to wander aimlessly amid the rows and hedges of a nominalist, fragmented shadow world. Whenever Catholics feel lost in a maze of modernity or postmodernity and are tempted to break off participation in the procession, to withdraw into a total rejection of contemporary science, scholarship, and art, we need to recall, with Flannery O'Connor, that a procession is not a march or regimented parade.[37] These latter the Church saw as Pelagian efforts to march mechanically with a false conviction that human progress has replaced Divine Providence: ever forwards never backwards or sideways. In comparison with such marches processions tend to meander depending upon countless interactions of the participants, each moving in answer to a divine call to follow the teacher Christ Jesus.

Like processions coming up against unexpected obstacles, Catholicism has to improvise and meander around the obstacles, oppositions, and delays. Is this not the way that God has created the universe? Do not contemporary scientists and artists confirm the wisdom of St. Thomas Aquinas, echoing the Fathers, that creation is a "procession" rather than a mechanistic, clocklike march? The mechanistic rationalism of the recent

---

35 See J. Boler, *Charles Peirce and Scholastic Realism* (Seattle: University of Washington Press, 1963); Karl-Otto Apel, *Charles Peirce: From Pragmatism to Pragmaticism* (Atlantic Highlands, N.J.: Humanities Press, 1995).

36 See Vincent Potter, "Objective Chance: Lonergan and Peirce on Scientific Generalization," in his *Peirce's Philosophical Perspectives* (Bronx, N.Y.: Fordham University Press, 1993); also Michael Forest, "Lonergan and the Classical American Tradition," in *Method: A Journal of Lonergan Studies* 23, no. 1 (2005): 17–42.

37 See Arthur Kennedy, "A Hope Embodied in Story: Flannery O'Connor's Vision," in *Lonergan Workshop* 4, 1984; "'The Good under Construction': Flannery O'Connor's Gift," in *College of Saint Thomas Magazine*, Autumn 1989; "Processions Are Our Rightful Home," commencement address, University of St. Thomas graduation, December 16, 1994.

past does not do justice to reason; the divine order of creation consists in its procession from God and return to him.

Given sin and the massive injustices in human history, the importance of holiness and the theological virtues cannot be overestimated in the task of participating in this Catholic procession as the Church makes her way during the third millennium. The fact that theology has disappeared from the cultural patrimony of our post-Enlightenment intellectual establishment has meant that the human sciences are bereft of a wisdom they desperately need. Empirical human sciences chart how human beings behave, how they act. They tend to take that behavior—no matter how disordered and sinful it is—as normative. On the basis of such studies social policies are formulated, and so the disorder and sin are structured into the society and culture in such laws as those condoning and supporting contraception, abortion, euthanasia, same-sex marriage, etc.

As St. Augustine reminds us, in such cycles of social and cultural decline, the intellectually virtuous tend toward cynicism, while the morally virtuous tend toward either a stoic withdrawal or epicurean distraction. The millennial challenge Catholicism poses to American culture today is to recover the full sweep of intelligence and reason in its quest for the whole truth about nature, man, and the Triune God.

CHAPTER 3

American Nominalism and the Need for a Science of Theology

PETER AUGUSTINE LAWLER
Berry College

MY PURPOSE here is to show how Pope Benedict XVI's defense of a true science of theology applies to the United States of America.[1] That defense is, finally, of the reasonableness of belief in a personal God who is rational, creative, and erotic. It requires going beyond the Regensburg lecture to the Pope's pathbreaking encyclical on love and to places in his writings where he makes clear that the fundamental human choice is not so much between reason and revelation as between the impersonal Logos, or God of the classical philosophers, and the personal Logos, or God described by the early Christians. The argument concerning which of those reasonable choices is more reasonable was what animated the study of the science of theology in the time of Hellenic Christianity. For us Americans, the greatness and the relevance of this philosopher-theologian-pope are in his articulation of a theory or science commensurate with the great practical achievement of our Founders, who, as the American Catholic political thinker John Courtney Murray claimed,

[1] I read the following by Ratzinger/Benedict to prepare for writing this essay: Pope Benedict XVI, "Faith, Reason and the University: Memories and Reflections" (lecture, University of Regensburg, Germany, September 12, 2006); the encyclical on love, *Deus Caritas Est*, December 25, 2005; Cardinal Joseph Ratzinger, *Introduction to Christianity* (San Francisco: Ignatius Press, 1994); Cardinal Joseph Ratzinger, *In the Beginning . . . A Catholic Understanding of the Story of Creation and the Fall* (Grand Rapids, Mich.: Eerdmans, 2005); and most of the writings and speeches contained in *The Essential Pope Benedict XVI*, ed. John Thornton and Susan Varenne (New York: HarperCollins, 2007), especially "On the Theological Basis of Prayer and Liturgy" (chap. 19) and "Truth and Freedom" (chap. 35), which were particularly important in shaping my argument.

built better than they knew. I'm dispensing with formality here, hoping not to rely on authority as much as to speak the truth. In my effort to do so, I gratefully acknowledge a debt to Joseph Ratzinger (Pope Benedict XVI) that could not be captured by any number of footnotes.

Even though the modern world has been characterized by de-Christianization and de-Hellenization, that does not mean it is fundamentally anti-Christian or anti-Greek. We speak more of the dignity or autonomy of the human person than ever. And we certainly have more confidence in and are more dependent on the science we have inherited from the Greeks than ever. Modern de-Hellenization has been largely animated by the desire to free the willful God and willful human person made in his image from being distorted or annihilated in the impersonal metaphysical system of Aristotle or some other philosopher or scientist. Modern de-Christianization has been largely animated by the desire to free science from all anthropomorphic or personal distortion in order to fuel real progress toward a certain understanding of the genuinely universal structure of reality, the goal of science first articulated, quite imperfectly, by the classical Greek philosophers. De-Christianization has been pursued on behalf of the free person, and de-Hellenization on behalf of impersonal science. They have been operating simultaneously and at cross-purposes.

The truth is that our world is in some ways both more personal and more impersonal, more Christian and more Greek, than ever. The distance between our personal experiences and what we think we know through science has never been wider. Without admitting it, we have abandoned the true goal of science, which is to give an account of the way all things, including human beings, are. We do not really believe we can reason about the true situation of the only being in the world, the human person, who is open to the truth about nature. We think we can know everything but the being who can know. We do not deny that such a personal being exists, whatever our scientists may teach. We do not even begin to try to lose our puny selves in some impersonal system or pantheistic reverie. Such denial is for Buddhists, with their amazing self-discipline. For now the phrase "Western Buddhist" remains an oxymoron.

It is especially apparent that we Americans see ourselves both more personally and more impersonally than ever. Virtually all sophisticated Americans claim to believe that Darwin teaches the whole truth about who or what we are. For Darwin, the individual human being exists only to serve the human species. Even our supersmart species has no enduring significance in the accidental evolutionary process. It is true both that I am nothing but species fodder and that what I, in particular, do has less than negligible significance for our species' future. Natural selection depends on the average, anonymous behavior of a huge number of members of any particular species. The individual or person and his illusory concerns about his personal significance mean nothing or are nothing. Even the genes that I so dutifully spread are soon dispersed into insignificance.

The same sophisticated Americans who pride themselves on being whole-hog Darwinians speak incessantly about the freedom and dignity of the individual and are proud of their freedom to choose. The particularly modern source of pride remains personal freedom from all authority, including the authority of God and nature. Our professed confidence in the reality of that freedom may be stronger than ever today. Even our Neo-Darwinian scientists, such as Daniel Dennett, who think there's no foundation for the idea of human dignity in what we know through science, admit it would be a disaster if they could really convince us to stop taking our dignity seriously. Certainly one piece of evidence that we are not living in genuinely reasonable times is that most sophisticated Americans seem unable to join Dennett in recognizing the laughable contradiction in their official self-understanding as autonomous chimps.

We Americans, in fact, are so unscientific that we do not even try to account for what we can see with our own eyes. Culturally speaking, we are divided into Darwin affirmers and Darwin deniers, into those who say that his theory of evolutionary natural selection can explain everything and those who say it explains nothing. Anybody should be able to see that the truth lies somewhere in between those two extremes.

The Darwin affirmers provide the best evidence around today that what Darwin teaches could not possibly be completely true. They tend to think of themselves so thoroughly as autonomous individuals that often they do not seek the natural fulfillment that comes through spreading their genes, through having kids. They are not doing their duty to their species by generating their replacements. They are even doing everything they can in the most scientific way not to have to be replaced. They think being itself will be extinguished if and when they die. Can Darwin explain why healthy members of a species enjoying the most favorable of environments would suddenly and quite consciously just decide to stop reproducing? It seems that members of a species smart enough and curious enough to have discovered the theory of natural selection are acting to make that theory untrue.

Meanwhile, our Evangelical and orthodox believers come much closer to living the way nature intends for our species to flourish. They pair-bond or marry, have lots of kids, raise them well, and then step aside for their natural replacements without inordinate resistance. What the Evangelicals and Mormons believe is better for our species' future than what the Neo-Darwinians believe. Examining this behavior, a Neo-Darwinian genuinely concerned for our species' future might insist that evolution not be taught in our schools. Nor can our sociobiologists explain why those Americans who believe that, as persons made in the image of a supernatural God, their true home is somewhere else are most at home in this world as citizens, friends, neighbors, parents, and children.

Still, our Evangelicals tend to join both those who speak of their autonomy and our Darwinians in believing that there is no support in nature at all for their purpose-driven lives. If it were not for the absolute truth of the Bible, they assert, something like aimless or relativistic naturalism would be true. They often present the human choice as between two competing worldviews, and reason has little to say about how to make that choice. Our Evangelicals often give themselves far too little credit. Their criticism of our libertarian autonomy freaks and our Darwinians would retain plenty of force even if they lost faith in the God of the Bible.

Our libertarians, our Darwinians, and our Evangelicals all agree that there is no science of theology. Reason, they insist, can't give us any understanding on who or what God is in a way that would provide actual guidance for our lives. They do not believe that we are hardwired, so to speak, to know the Logos who, or which, is the source of our freedom and our openness to the truth about all things. Libertarians and Evangelicals both believe that the free person is real, but they do not believe that there is any support in nature for his existence. Darwinians, quite unrealistically, deny what anyone can see with his own eyes about personal or individual behavior. Because we all refuse to believe in the possibility of a science of theology, we all lack a way of talking reasonably about the real lives of particular human persons.

We do not live in a very reasonable time because we are governed by a particular cultural or historical choice to limit the domain of reason over our lives. This modern self-limitation, as I will explain, was quite understandable. But we now know from experience that the simultaneous attempts to free faith from science or philosophy and science from faith have produced undignified, self-mutilated lives. Most fundamentally, we seem not to be courageous enough to live well with what we know. The truth is that the modern view of reason is quite questionable. It is, thank God, far from the last word on what we can know.

The Science of Theology: Hellenic Christianity versus Classical Philosophy

To free us from the delusion that we have that last word on reason, we return to the first words about the relationship between Greek philosophy or science and Christianity spoken during the period of Hellenic Christianity. Then, the Greeks and the Christians agreed that we are hardwired as beings with minds to think about who or what God must be and that we are animated by eros, or love, to seek the truth about God. The idea that God is Logos is what allowed the Greeks and the Christians to use both argument and mockery to collaborate against those religions that are obviously unreasonable and man-made. God is neither cruel nor arbitrary, and the truth about God must correspond to what we can know about ourselves and the rest of nature according to our best lights. Both the Greeks and the Christians contributed to genuine enlightenment, to the liberation of human beings from the confines of merely civil or political theology, from a world where the Word of God both was used as a weapon and justified the use of weapons.

Through reflection, Aristotle attempted to grasp God as the object of every human desire or love. He understood God only as the object of love, as a wholly self-sufficient or unerotic or unmovable being, not as a person at all. Aristotle's God is certainly not a "relational" God, one who cares or even knows about the existence of particular human beings. According to Aristotle, our pursuit of divine knowledge, or what God knows, becomes progressively more impersonal. The pursuit of philosophic or scientific truth requires that the individual philosopher die to himself. The Socratic drama of the pursuit of wisdom is the particular being losing himself in his apprehension of anonymous or impersonal truth.

From this view, we approach divinity, or what is best in us, through our perception of the logos, or rational causality that governs all things. We see past every anthropomorphic claim for personal intervention or personal causation that would disrupt that logos. From this liberated view, the idea of a personal God is an oxymoron. It is, in fact, a repulsive denial of the responsibility of theological science and science generally.

The Christian criticism of Aristotelian theology is that it does not account for what we really know about the human person. For the Greek philosophers, the realm of human freedom, finally, is a mythical idea, one that must be rhetorically supported but for which there is no scientific evidence. The only freedom is the freedom of the human mind from anthropomorphic delusions about natural causation. The Christians respond that human longings and human action exhibit evidence of personal freedom, and the person must have some actual foundation in being itself. What we do know, they say, points in the direction of the creative activity of a personal God. The personalities of God and man cannot be wholly or irredeemably unrelated. The possibility of the free and rational being open to the truth depends upon the corresponding possibility of a personal, rational science of theology.

The classical philosophers were, of course, perfectly aware that human beings are "manly," that they need to feel important. Such self-confidence is required to make self-conscious life endurable and great human deeds possible. But according to their science, all assertions of human importance are unrealistic exaggerations, and the philosopher gently mocks without obviously undermining the aspirations of particular individuals to self-sufficiency. For the Christians, however, even science depends upon the possibility of personal significance, and Christian theology criticizes both the civil theology and the natural theology of the Greeks and Romans for their inability to account for personal freedom, for the being who is not fundamentally merely part of a city or part of some necessitarian natural whole. According to the Christians, not only do particular men and women need to feel important; they are, in fact, important. The Christians add that the unrealistic exaggerations of their magnanimous pretensions need, in fact, the chastening of the truthful virtue of humility, the virtue of ineradicably relational and lovingly dependent beings.

That there is a ground for personal freedom in an otherwise seemingly necessitarian cosmos does, in some ways, offend the mind, but to understand all that exists in terms of impersonal causation suggests that Being itself is constituted by an intelligence that is incapable of comprehending itself. The human being, the being who can understand Being, seems to be a chance occurrence in a cosmos that has no particular need for and is seemingly distorted by his existence. The appearance of the human person, even the philosopher with the name Socrates, necessarily offends the human mind in some ways, but as far as we know, the human mind can only appear or function in a whole person. The real existence of the whole philosopher or physicist cannot be accounted for in any mathematical or certainly necessitarian physics. So in some ways it might offend the person's reason less to affirm an account of the precondition and ground of all being to be creative and truly conscious, or erotic and rational, thinking. The world, in the final analysis, is more love than mathematics, and the particular human person is more significant and wonderful than the stars.

The Greeks focus on the eternity, the Christians on the loving creativity of God. For the Christians, the God who is the ultimate source of our being is animated, as we are, by logos and eros. The source of our being is someone who cannot be reduced to mind or will or even some theoretical combination of the two. Made in his image, we personal, erotic, and knowing beings cannot be reduced to mind or will or body or even some abstract combination of the three. One aspect of the reasonableness of faith is its perception of the intrinsic link between God's love and the whole reality of human life.

The philosophic or scientific understanding of the world in terms of impersonal necessity or eternity alone cannot account for the real existence of persons, of beings open to the truth and defined in this world by time. The eternal God of the Greeks has no relationship to the temporal, and the dependence and incompleteness of time-bound beings mean nothing to him. Insofar as human beings are moved by his existence, it is in pursuit of self-sufficient freedom from who they really are. If time and eternity really are infinitely distant from one another, then we cannot understand why human beings can know God or anything eternal.

Classical monotheism, in truth, denies the real relationships between God and man and between eternity and time. It may, in fact, culminate in the conclusion that the only thing a human being can know for certain is that he is not eternal, that he is some kind of chance occurrence soon to be extinguished in a necessitarian cosmos. Greek philosophers clearly distinguished the personal illusion of religion from the philosophic science of theology, showing that, for the most part, at least the lives of particular men are as unreal or as insignificant as the personal gods they invent. For the Greeks, religion was useful for the regulation of lives, but it has nothing to do with the truth.

From the Greek view, the early Christians seemed like atheists. They rejected the whole world of ancient religion and its gods as nothing but empty custom or contrary to what we can really know. That is because the Christians agreed with the Greek philosophers that traditional myth must be rejected in favor of the truth about Being, and the Christians added that all human beings are called to regulate their lives in light of what they can really know. Only from the perspective of a personal logos can the truth affirm and guide human freedom. The Christians, by discovering a transformed understanding of the logos at the ground of Being, showed God to be a Person concerned with persons. The Christians show why divine truth cannot be separated from personal morality.

From the perspective of the distinctive reasonableness of Christian faith, man's inner openness to God comes from what he knows about himself as a relational being, as a person who knows and loves other "whos." The philosophical view of God is that our thoughts or minds alone are divine, and the mind detached from the whole human being is less a who than a what. The Christian view is that we are made in God's image as whole rational and erotic beings; not just thought but love is divine. The standard of moral judgment is what we cannot help but know about our personhood or creatureliness, about the responsibilities that flow from personal awareness of loving dependence. Sin flows from the denial of the truth about our freedom, from the madness that flows from the aspiration to be as autonomous or self-sufficient as some thinkers imagine God to be. The sin described in Genesis flows from the false separation of divine wisdom from personal or "relational" morality.

In the Hellenic world, the science of theology was always reasonable without achieving rational certainty. The truth is that the arguments for the Christian and the Greek accounts of the logos at the ground of Being both have problems. Christianity's view that what we can know about the human person reasonably points in the direction of a personal logos does not eradicate the apparent *mystery* of personal freedom in a world seemingly governed by natural necessity. If the mystery is real, the Greek philosophers argued, science becomes impossible. The Christian response that without that mystery there would be nobody to know scientific truth does not completely answer that objection. Nor could the Christians dispel all questions about why a wholly self-sufficient and rational God completely ungoverned by time and chance would become a Creator. How can it be that such a God is erotic or animated by a passionate sense of incompleteness?

And, of course, some Christians wondered whether the Hellenizing of Christianity through the emphasis on God as Logos chained him, in effect, to natural laws that were not his creation. The emphasis on either God's love or God's reason can easily seem to compromise the freedom of his will and so the omnipotence on which our hopes for personal salvation rest. Arguably that emphasis also undermined the freedom of the will of the persons made in his image. The limiting of the willful God with either logos or love seems to undermine his personal significance, and so ours.

Modern Nominalism

It's understandable why there were Christian efforts to liberate God from science, from the constraints of reason. The most obvious efforts came from late-medieval nominalism. Words are names, nothing more, it asserted. Our speech, or logos, does not give us access to the way God or nature is. The Word of God is pure will, and the word of man, who is made in his image, is also pure will. Words, for us, are merely weapons because we are not hardwired to discover the truth about God, nature, or each other through reason. This nominalist conclusion was, in effect, affirmed by the leaders of the Reformation. They, too, meant to free the personal experience of the living God from the cold constraints of reason. Our direct (really, private) personal experience of his will and his love eludes every impersonal system. The living, giving God, the Reformers believed, is nothing like Aristotle's God.

By freeing the person from logos, the combined effects of voluntarism and the Reformation were to deny the possibility of a science of theology. And so they also freed science from any concern with God, allowing it to focus exclusively on what we can know with certainty, the mathematically expressed laws of matter in motion. To know with certainty is to know without any personal distortion. Modern science becomes more openly impersonal than its ancient predecessor because Aristotelian theology left too much room for science's personal distortion and directed the mind toward uncertain speculation. The aim of modern physics, ultimately, is the same as that of ancient physics, to show that the world is the home of the human mind.

Now we can finally turn to how the nominalist denial of the science of theology shaped the early modern liberalism, the Lockeanism, that, in turn, shaped both the American founding and the individualistic dynamic of American history. For Locke, we experience ourselves as free individuals or persons, but there is no divine or natural support for our personhood or individuality. Nature is utterly indifferent to my personal existence, so I have to establish my personal significance, my very being as a free individual, in opposition to that indifference. From my individual view, nature is worthless, and according to nature, I am worthless.

The detachment of the person from nature or from logos, in the name of freedom and in the name of science, allows us to experience ourselves as pure freedom or pure selfishness. There's no evidence, in fact, for an active or giving Creator, no evidence that God or nature provides for the person in any way. Our personal freedom, like God's, is utterly mysterious: there's no evident natural or divine foundation for *me*, for my being. So I have to establish and expand my freedom—my very being—on my own, through my own willful work. I have to create or constitute myself out of nothing, as God allegedly created the whole world.

Like the Christians and against the Greeks, we Americans assert that each particular person is equally and infinitely significant. From the perspective of the person, from my perspective, nothing is more important than the security, significance, and happiness that characterize *my* existence. Each person or individual exists for himself, not genuinely in a dependent and loving relationship with others. Love of God or other human persons is for suckers. It's undignified for me not to tell the truth about how contingent and self-determined my own being is.

The idea of God remains in Locke in the form of Deism, which is, in part, a revival of the ancient rejection of an active, personal God. Locke's "Nature's God" is a past-tense God. Deism also has some connection with the Pascalian view of the mysterious hiddenness of God. Certainly Locke's God is not quite the impersonal God of Aristotle, because the former's affirmation of the reality of the mystery of the free human person points in some sense to a mysterious Creator. But that Creator does not show himself as a person to us. We act as suckers when we think of ourselves as creatures, as in some way gratefully dependent on or personally connected to his providence. Our Lockean Declaration of Independence, we remember, speaks of a Creator but never of creatures.

For Locke, words, our capacity for reasonable speech or logos, do not give us any access to the truth about nature or God. There is, in fact, no science of theology. Words are the weapons we use to secure our being against nature and without God. Words are the weapons we use to make ourselves progressively freer or progressively more real. Locke's state of nature, for example, was not meant to be an empirical account of the way human beings are. It distorts and exaggerates our personal or individual freedom. The state of nature was a tool used by Locke to liberate the individual from nature and from other individuals.

The Lockean individual is itself a weapon, a willful invention abstracted from the whole, relational truth about the human person. Proof of our freedom is our power to make that abstraction more real over time. Locke himself was all for limited government, but his project was hardly limited to government. He aimed, with great success, to reconstruct every human relationship and institution with the free or selfishly calculating individual in mind. As the Supreme Court said in *Lawrence v. Texas*, our Framers deliberately gave the word "liberty" no definite, stable content so that it could be used as a weapon for each generation of Americans to advance the cause of individual liberation or autonomy. What seems like necessary and proper limits to liberty to one generation of Americans seems like despotism to the next. Marriage, we now are coming to think, is a free contract between any two individuals for any purpose at all; it has been freed from any necessary connection to our biological purposes and limitations.

Locke's individual is free to view the wholly impersonal or mathematical nature that the scientists can comprehend and control as a resource for their personal disposal. He is even free to think of his own body in that way. His view of his freedom from nature even allows him to be critical scientifically of the impersonal pretensions of science. If it is true that there is no necessary connection between the free, willful individual and the natural order, then there is no reason to believe that we can comprehend the order of nature except by bringing it under our personal control.

Locke to Marx: History Replaces Nature

Freeing the person from nature necessarily personalizes what we can actually know about nature. We can only know what we have made in our own image. The purpose of our reason is to will personal reality into being. So all science, all human knowledge, must finally be technological; technology or history, the names we give to what we have made for ourselves, even seems to be all there is. The detachment of the person from nature frees the individual to impose his desire for personal significance on nature. We are free to replace impersonal natural evolution, which means nothing to us, with conscious and volitional evolution, human effort with the indefinite perpetuation of each infinitely significant individual in mind. And the science of theology, which aims at orthodoxy, is replaced by orthopraxis; there is no truth but who and what we have made for ourselves.

It is a pretty small step from Locke to Marx, from the view that the individual is free to constitute himself to the "historical" view that he is free to constitute all there is. The detachment of science from all concern with theology eventually seems to lead to the replacement of natural science by historical science, to Marx's description of the impending total victory of human freedom over nature and God. The separation of eternity (impersonal natural science) from time (the free person or individual) at the beginning of the modern world is resolved, according to Marx, by the victory of time. Human freedom or history frees each of us from the tyranny of the indifference of eternal necessity.

There are many problems with this conclusion. To begin with, if history is a science, then logos once again seems to reign at the expense of the freedom or significance of particular persons. It does not matter what I really intend to do; my personal actions only have significance as part of a whole, a historical future, beyond my comprehension and control. Those who really believed history is a science were all too ready to sacrifice today's individuals for a historical perfection nobody living will ever see or enjoy. From a Lockean view, those who gave their lives to history were suckers, and those who were murdered on behalf of history were denied their personal dignity.

The tyranny of Marxists can be traced to the detachment of the abstraction "history" from the lives of particular persons or individuals. As history became a scientific replacement for modern natural science, it became just as impersonal or systematic as modern science. Hegel and Marx even wrote of "the end of history," of history as a time-bound logos of temporal beings. The great Marxist/Hegelian Alexandre Kojève explained that the end of history would have to be the end of "man properly so-called," the disappearance of the personal being free from nature's domination. The end of history, according to Kojève, would be the victory of eternity over the temporary aberration of time. The human species would be reintegrated into nature with all the others, and there would be no one left to know the truth about the impersonal natural necessity that would once again be the truth, and nothing but.

To be fair to Marx (as opposed to being fair to Marxist tyrants), he, quite incoherently, thought that the end of history or communism would be the free flourishing of individuality unconstrained by natural necessity or any other form of alienation. It is hard to know why Marx called communism "communism," because in such a society we would be completely free from all relational obsessions, such as love, that would limit our freedom. The freedom won by human beings from nature and from each other under communism would remain, with the addition of liberation from the division of labor, from being compelled to work for others. Under communism, freedom would be just another word for nothing left that we *have* to do.

Our most astute libertarians today are beginning to see that Marx is their friend, once he is stripped of insane and dangerous hopes such as the inevitability of revolution and the actual end of history. The world he worked for is the one today's libertarians celebrate as having largely arrived—the one with a huge and ever-expanding menu of choices for liberated individuals. Marx thought capitalism liberated women to be wage slaves just like men. Our libertarians tweak that observation by saying women are now free to seek self-fulfillment however they please, just like men, and the opportunities for work from which they have to choose are often challenging and enjoyable. There is no denying, in fact, that the achievements of modern technology in liberating lots of ordinary persons from scarcity and drudgery are wonderful revelations about what free beings can do here and now to improve their conditions.

Marx and our libertarians agree that the technological conquest of scarcity liberates the individual for "a menu of choices." But that liberation from God, nature, and even other people means that the personal is deprived of all guidance about how to choose. All choice that does not concern survival becomes a preference, a whim, so our freedom becomes nothing more than anarchy or pure indeterminacy. I can be anything I want to be, I say, but nothing I choose has genuine weight or significance. So the person, as the existentialists whine, comes to be seen as nothing more than an absurd leftover, an accidental aberration, from the impersonal natural necessity that governs the rest of existence.

The truth is that the person cannot constitute himself out of nothing, and the abstract individual Locke invented with that capability always falls short of becoming anywhere near completely real. We cannot remake all of reality in our image; the more we comprehend through control, the more we are aware of the infinite spaces that continue to elude us. The more we experience ourselves as free or disconnected individuals, the more we experience the mysterious contingency of our very beings. We still have bodies and we still die, and in fact we are more death haunted than ever. We still cannot help falling in love, though we Lockeans and Darwinians and Marxists have no idea how to talk about love. All our personal efforts to secure our beings have made us too anxious and disoriented, too lonely and personally insignificant, to be at home in the technological world we have created to replace our clearly inadequate natural home.

Nihilism or Relativism

Without any connection to a personal reality, a personal logos, beyond his own making, sometimes it seems that the free being cannot endure. Today, we allegedly autonomous persons are so conscious of the limits of our biological existence that we seem incapable of creating anything that can stand the test of time. And in our time, Marx's historical science has been replaced by nihilism or techno-relativism. We cannot even pretend to speak more than whimsically about anything that does not contribute to our futile efforts at survival. The only real morality we have left—morality reduced to safe sex or, more generally, safe choice—has nothing to do with the significance of the person's existence. Our proud claim that something real distinguishes the person from natural necessity seems more questionable than ever.

Nihilism is the view that what distinguishes me from the rest of nature means nothing or is nothing. It means that "I," the particular person, am nothing. The time after the discrediting of Locke and Marx should, from one nihilistic view, belong to Darwin or to the revelation of the complete truth of his impersonal science. Sober Darwinians agree with whiny existentialists that the Lockean individual is absurd. There is no natural or real evidence for his existence. Surely it is ridiculous to claim the individual was somehow just dropped into nature to go to war against it like some crazed parasitic predator. The Darwinian adds that nature really does intend all animals, even us, to be basically happy or content. So we have acquired through natural selection instincts that produce pleasure in us when we do our duties as social beings; we have a natural moral sense. If we really were to detach ourselves from those instincts, we would condemn ourselves to the futile pursuit of happiness that ends only in death.

The Darwinian concludes that the Lockean individual—the individual free from nature—is nothing but a misery-producing delusion. Surely the Darwinian is right that nature provides us lots of guidance when it comes to happiness. It is still the case in our individualistic time that most people claim they are happiest as members of families, and our natural longings really do point most of us in the direction of doing what it takes to keep the species going. So, thoughtful Darwinians claim that they have the antidote to the nihilism of individualism. Nature gives us guidance concerning the point of our lives, and we find fulfillment and happiness in doing what we are inclined to do by nature.

But the Lockean can reasonably respond that Darwinism is nihilism. The impersonal truth is that I exist for the species, not for myself, and what I do as a particular individual means nothing or is nothing. Darwin cannot explain why members of only one species can think so abstractly and imaginatively that they conceive of themselves as individuals. Nor can Darwin explain why members of only one species are in full technological rebellion against nature. In Harvey Mansfield's analysis, the conviction that Darwin might teach the truth about the chance and necessity that govern every life might well have been the main cause of the "manliness run amok" of the twentieth century, just as it might be the cause of the biotechnology run amok of the twenty-first. People are more concerned than ever about their personal significance, their importance or status, their very being as particular persons, in our officially egalitarian time.

What we know is that the Lockean criticism of Darwin from the perspective of human freedom contains much truth. And the Darwinian criticism of Locke from the perspective of the natural goods connected with our embodiment is also largely true. Both these criticisms are true because the Lockeans and Darwinians both think too abstractly. They share the error of unrealistic abstractness because they agree that there is no natural support for human freedom. They also agree on what human nature is; what the Lockeans call human freedom has no natural or real support at all. Words are not meant to give us any access to the truth about nature. For the Lockeans, they are weapons for individual preservation and flourishing, and for Darwinians they are for the preservation and flourishing of the species. We are certainly not hardwired to know any personal reality that we did not make for ourselves, including, of course, God.

The American Need for a Science of Theology

We are, despite our proud enlightenment, much more a willful than a reasonable people. We believe that we are perfectly free to deny what we can know and even or especially to deny that we know it. We claim to be free to find it comfortable to believe that we are really autonomous chimps. We are free, we believe, to choose personal reality over scientific truth, distorting science to serve a freedom that our scientists do not acknowledge as real. But one sign of our true dignity, our true freedom as rational, erotic, creative, and relational beings, is that we still know that it is degrading to prefer comfort to truth. Our attempts to live without being moved by love and death (because they are more trouble than they are worth) mainly produce not some less-than-personal apathetic passivity but chaotic, angry disorientation.

Our Founders, our political Fathers, clearly privileged personal reality over impersonal science, and so they built better—they were more Christian—than they knew. They sometimes thought of themselves as proponents of the light of science and "Nature's God" against the monkish ignorance and superstition of Christians. But for them science served, above all, human freedom. And that freedom is nothing like the Epicurean serenity that Jefferson claimed to have privately enjoyed or the rational acceptance of nature's indifference to Jefferson's personal significance. Our Fathers' service to the significance of the person or the individual is what saves them from all charges of capitalism, materialism, atheism, and so forth. Surely, most of our Fathers most of the time would have laughed at the Epicureans or Marxists or Darwinians who claimed that they were, in truth, slaves to forces beyond their personal control.

Americans may justly be criticized for sometimes regarding even other persons as natural resources to be exploited. But they are rarely so materialistic as to forget that it is a free being that is doing the exploiting. They can also be criticized for alienating themselves even from their own bodies, but that is because they think of themselves as something other than bodies. Our pragmatism is not materialism, because it depends on our conviction that our freedom is somehow real. The free being who secures himself as something more than a body is the one, as Alexis de Tocqueville (author of the best book on Americans, *Democracy in America*) explains, who freely pursues enjoyment but never takes time to surrender to actual, instinctual enjoyment. Americans, in a way, exhibit the extreme opposite of nihilistic behavior; they work hard to avoid the conclusion that their very being is nothing.

Not only that, our Fathers deliberately did not make it clear whether the person they served is the creature described by Protestant Christians or the free individual described by Locke. Either way, they served the dignity of the person free from natural and political domination. Our Lockeans and Protestants ally against the impersonal natural science that denies the free will or free choice of the particular person or individual. Whether Protestant or Lockean, we understand ourselves as mysteriously free from nature. And either way we are way too sure that there is no science of theology.

Whether Protestant or Lockean, we cannot really claim that our way of life is particularly reasonable. As Tocqueville explains, our Christianity saves us from the manliness run amok, producing the view that anything might be done for some futuristic historical utopia. It also teaches us that we have moral duties in common and even that we were made for more than mere survival. But religion achieves these beneficial goals, Tocqueville adds, only by being exempted, without discussion, from our habitual critical scrutiny. Americans, in the name of moral freedom and just sanity itself, decide not to think about the most important questions concerning personal significance, including, of course, about God. So, in some deep way, both our religion and our incessant labor to secure our being seem to be diversions from what we really know. They both oppose human freedom to what we can know through science.

But what we know through science also seems to be a diversion from what we experience about our freedom. Our physicists can explain everything about the cosmos but the strange behavior of physicists. And our Neo-Darwinian biologists do not even try to begin to explain their joyful discovery of the truth about all things as the product of tools for species flourishing. Everyone knows our scientists are self-forgetful and that they have little real to say about who human persons are. Certainly they cannot explain why the Americans who believe that their true home is somewhere else are the ones most at home in this world or why those who say they believe that they are as at home here as members of any other species are most in rebellion against their social instincts and biological limitations.

Americans are caught between incompatible diversions because de-Hellenization has defended our freedom, our autonomy, so well against impersonal science, and de-Christianization has emptied our freedom of any real or "transcendent" content. The result is that we live in unstable, disorienting, narcissistic, degrading, and impersonal times, and we wonder whether the freedom our Fathers worked so hard and well to secure is either real or worth defending. But our return to the time of the Hellenic Christians reminds us that the sundering of the person from logos was a very questionable historical decision, one that artificially and futilely limited the scope of human reason. As far as we can tell, logos must be personal; only persons are rational, erotic, and relational enough to be open to the truth about all things, and only persons have the significance that comes with living freely, responsibly, and lovingly with what they know. A wholly necessitarian or impersonal world of minds and bodies would not be known by anyone at all. The modern diversions are the results of thinking unrealistically or abstractly about who we and God really are. It really is true that the beginning of the cure for what ails us Americans is more science, not less. Our Holy Father points us in the direction of the theory, culminating in the science of theology, adequate to the great success of the experiment in freedom of our political Fathers.

CHAPTER 4

Christianity and Modern Liberty: What Kind of Accommodation?*

DANIEL J. MAHONEY
Assumption College

IN DECISIVE respects the West is a civilization shaped by its Christian inheritance. It owes to Christianity and the Christian spirit the separation of the things of Caesar and the things of God, the exalted place of conscience in its moral life, and its rejection of the monstrous and idolatrous Pharaonic state. But the West is much more than the "Old West," to adopt the revealing term of Danish historian David Gress. The "New West," the West that arose out of the Enlightenment, above all values science, technological progress, and human rights. It grows evermore estranged from its Christian and classical sources. We are confronted by this paradox: the "democratic revolution" of which Tocqueville was the prophet and diagnostician owes *something* to Christianity, especially its unequivocal affirmation of human dignity, even as it erodes the Christian foundations of Western civilization.

At the same time, confronted by totalitarianism and other manifestations of modern nihilism, liberals and religious believers have found new reasons to see beyond past antagonisms. In his remarkable 1960 Eddington lecture, "Beyond Nihilism," the Hungarian-born chemist and philosopher Michael Polanyi fully anticipated our situation. "The churches," he wrote, "seemed to recall modern man from a state beyond nihilism to his condition before the secular enlightenment." Yet modern man, democratic

* This essay is a significantly revised and abridged version of chapter 2, "Beyond Nihilism: Religion, Liberty, and the Art of Mediation", of my recently published book, *The Conservative Foundations of the Liberal Order: Defending Democracy against Its Modern Enemies and Immoderate Friends* (Wilmington, Del.: ISI Books, 2010). It is published in its present form with permission of ISI Books.

man, rightly rejects the authoritarian imposition of religion and does not wish "to go back on the scientific revolution which has secularized extensive domains of knowledge." We do not wish to go back, but we can no longer rest comfortably with the modernist and postmodernist severing of truth and liberty, and also freedom and the moral contents of life. In this reflection I will explore the multiple dimensions of this problematic with the help of two contemporary students of the "theological-political problem" in its Western form, the American political theorist Mark Lilla and the French political philosopher Pierre Manent.

The Great Separation

If Pierre Manent insists that there can be no definitive solution to the theological-political problem, Mark Lilla calls for an uncompromising return to the secularist foundations of modern liberal democracy. In *The Stillborn God: Religion, Politics, and the Modern West*, a widely discussed work published in 2007, the American political theorist highlights the various contemporary threats to the "Great Separation" (I will follow him in capitalizing the phrase) between religion and politics that was theorized by Thomas Hobbes in the seventeenth century and that, with modifications, has become *the* basis of liberal constitutionalism in the Western world. For Lilla, the Great Separation is nothing less than the nonnegotiable foundation of modern liberty. His book gives learned, eloquent expression to what one might call *secular fundamentalism*—the belief that any public role for religion or religious affirmation threatens human liberty as well as the delicate "art of intellectual separation,"[1] as Lilla calls it—at the heart of the liberal order. By the latter phrase, Lilla means the separation of the politics and scientific inquiry from substantive ethical guidance, from any comprehensive account of the good life for human beings.

One defect of Lilla's book is that it treats liberal or constitutional democracy almost exclusively as an epiphenomenal expression of the categories and assumptions of early modern political philosophy. Lilla shows no interest in specifically *religious* arguments for freedom of conscience and the separation of church and state. He also ignores the perspective of democratic statesmen who drew upon Christian as well as modern philosophical sources in articulating the rights and duties of men and citizens. For example, the American Declaration of Independence famously invokes both "nature's God" and God as "Creator," "Providence," and "Supreme Judge"

[1] Mark Lilla, *The Stillborn God: Religion, Politics, and the Modern West* (New York: Knopf, 2007), p. 89. All subsequent references to *The Stillborn God* are cited parenthetically in the body of the text as *SG*.

of the world. It invokes "rights" but also speaks in a more traditional idiom of "prudence" and the requirements of personal and political "honor." With equal plausibility, it can be interpreted in light of modern Deism and the "state of nature" doctrine of Hobbes and Locke *and* in light of an older tradition of natural law and natural right. To do full justice to the statesman's perspective would invariably lead one to question the simplistic identification of liberty with radical secularism and hence the self-evidence of the Great Separation in its most doctrinaire contemporary forms.

Lilla is committed to a public sphere shorn of religion or any religiously inspired conceptions of the good life for human beings. He is a partisan, although a remarkably restrained one, of what Richard John Neuhaus called "the naked public square." At the same time, he is sensitive to the historically exceptional and fragile character of the "liberal" separation of religion and politics, power and opinion, truth and liberty. He believes that a political-theological nexus that expressly connects God, man, and the world better corresponds to the psychological needs and spiritual longings of human beings than the austere secularism demanded by the modern liberal order. For Lilla, the art of political and intellectual separation is a rare historical achievement that is vulnerable to criticism on philosophical, psychological, and political grounds. It has been subject to legitimate criticism from philosophical critics such as Rousseau, Kant, and nineteenth-century Romantics who lamented its soullessness—its heavy-handed abstraction from the spiritual and poetic sides of our humanity. And it is under increasing assault from the various fundamentalisms both in the West and in the Islamic world that demand a restoration of political theology—the full integration of religion and law—as the foundation of any viable human order.

Why then have I called Lilla's approach an exercise in secularist fundamentalism? To begin with, Lilla shares no small dose of the "anti-theological ire," as Leo Strauss called it, that distorted the Enlightenment's purportedly rational approach to the "theological-political problem." His moderate *tone*, his seemingly measured "cost-benefit analysis" of the human cost of the Great Separation, coexists with and gives way to an illiberal demand for unending vigilance against any political expression on the part of religious believers. He seems to forget that believers have long made their peace with liberal democracy (and in the American case played a major role in establishing democratic institutions in the first place). In addition, their publicly salutary insistence on justice and personal responsibility is inseparable from certain religious assumptions about man and the world. In this regard, Lilla is no less "authoritarian," no less committed to a rigorously naked public square than more openly aggressive theorists of liberal "neutrality" such as John Rawls and Richard Rorty.

The Arts of Mediation

As Ralph C. Hancock has written in a particularly penetrating critique of *The Stillborn God*, Lilla has no room for "the arts of mediation," theoretical and practical efforts to think together the human and divine realms without conflating them or denying the legitimate (even precious) autonomy of the political sphere of human existence. Lilla makes only two references in his book to Alexis de Tocqueville, the modern student of democracy most committed to a "mediation" that would modify and humanize the separation of religion and liberty. At the heart of Tocqueville's intellectual and political project was an effort to promote the blending of the "spirit of liberty" and the "spirit of religion" in a way appropriate to a modern democratic age. He did so in full awareness of the dangers inherent in the old regime's conflation of religious and political authority. He supported the separation of church and state as something that was good for both politics and religion even as he emphasized the need for a robust if *indirect* role for religion in democratic public life. Lilla tersely rules out this project, arguing that "accommodation is not understanding" (*SG*, 304). In response to this summary objection, Hancock raises the possibility of another approach that also surely deserves the appellation "liberal":

> Might we propose renewing the project of understanding the accommodation and drawing upon concrete achievements of reconciling political and religious goods, not to solve the problem but to refine and manage the claims of transcendence that must emerge in a substantially pluralistic society?[2]

Despite his apparent evenhandedness in addressing the human consequences of the Great Separation, Lilla dogmatically eschews the path of mediation. His analysis is in decisive respects frozen in time: the one thing most needful is said to be a return to the Hobbesian roots of liberal democracy. Hobbes's *Leviathan*, appropriately "liberalized" by his great political and philosophical successors such as John Locke and David Hume, provides the core, nonnegotiable assumptions of Lilla's analysis of the relationship between religion and politics in the modern world. It is the true alternative to every form of Romanticism, decisionism, and religious enthusiasm. For Lilla religion almost always connotes messianic expectations as well as the negation of reason. Not that he wants to defend every aspect of Hobbes's thinking. Lilla freely concedes that the English

[2] Ralph Hancock, "Back to Where We Started or the New Hobbism Comes Out," *Perspectives on Political Science* 38, no. 1 (Winter 2009): 15.

philosopher takes atheism for granted, that he goes too far in reducing religion to a merely anthropological phenomenon, that he unreasonably claims to have explained away the possibility of the self-revelation of a transcendent God (*SG*, 78, 89). But such seemingly insuperable obstacles to taking Hobbes seriously as a guide to the religious question are not allowed to get in Lilla's way.

With Hobbes, we are called to accept the self-evidence of a "morally mute natural world" and to "separate our investigations of nature from our thoughts about God or the duties of man" (*SG*, 89). Even if we have good reasons to quarrel *on rational grounds* with Hobbes's mechanistic and reductionist scientific "findings," we may still profitably welcome his project. Not only has it liberated politics from ecclesiastical control but it has freed intellectual inquiry from the intrusions of theological and metaphysical reflection altogether. In Lilla's presentation, Hobbes's ferocious assault on "the vast Kingdom of Darkness" is the necessary precondition for the modern secular university with its unending multiplication of autonomous disciplines and its rejection of any claim to unified truth about man or the Whole.

The Political Consequences of Hobbes

Lilla presents a limited, one-sided picture of what Bertrand de Jouvenel called "the political consequences of Hobbes" in an important chapter in his 1955 masterwork *Sovereignty*.[3] Jouvenel agrees with Leo Strauss and Michael Oakeshott that Hobbes is best understood as an individualist and liberal (or proto-liberal) thinker and not, as is commonly claimed, as the father of modern totalitarianism. Hobbes's defense of "absolute" authority is at the service of securing the life and liberty of individuals and not of promoting a cult of state power. Leviathan, that "mortal god" among men, is conceived not on the model of a totalitarian state but rather as an instrument for stopping "the mischief which the intersection of (men's) appetites may do them."[4] Hobbes's thought provides not only the theoretical inspiration for the radical separation of church and state but also the basic premises for modern political economy, that hedonistic "science" that identifies the goods of men with the things desired.

While Hobbes's assumptions are indeed liberal, individualistic, and hedonistic, they are ultimately incompatible with self-government in both the moral (the government of the self) and political (civic self-rule) understandings of the term. With Hobbes, "absolute libertarianism" gives rise not

[3] Bertrand de Jouvenel, *Sovereignty* (Indianapolis, Ind.: Liberty Fund, 1997), pp. 279–98.

[4] Ibid., p. 290.

only to hedonism and moral relativism but to authoritarianism as a necessary means for maintaining the fragile social tie. A hedonist society—a godless society—demands nothing less than a "strong and stable government."[5] Jouvenel argues, convincingly in my view, that political liberty depends upon more elevated suppositions about human nature—and more noble and generous tendencies in the human soul—than those allowed in the official "system" of Hobbes. Beyond the neutral art or science of intellectual separation Hobbes's political philosophy articulates and then builds upon a fearful and godless individualism. This individualism paradoxically has profoundly collectivist implications. Hobbes's philosophical and religious critics of old who derided "the monster of Malmsbury" in many cases had a deeper appreciation of the "political consequences" of his thought than the American political theorist fretting about the dangers posed by the "Christian Right" as he writes away in his study.

Lilla's selective appropriation of Hobbes is tied to a false dichotomy that structures his book as a whole. He repeatedly leaves his reader with a binary choice between "political theology" and the "Great Separation." We are said to live "on the other shore" (*SG*, 102) of that alternative since political theology is no longer a "living force" (*SG*, 103)—a viable option—in our Western democratic societies. Lilla never comes to terms with the full implications of insisting, dogmatically I might add, that we modern liberal democrats conceive political life "solely with reference to man" (*SG*, 90). He speaks of the need for human beings to take their bearings from this-worldly "lucidity" (*SG*, 309) but never specifies what is the source of that alleged clarity. For Lilla, human self-sovereignty is a more or less benign affair that has nothing to do with the temptation for human beings to turn themselves into gods. Ignoring the critique of unmitigated human self-sovereignty that is common to both Christian and "conservative liberal" critics of radical modernity, he blames twentieth-century totalitarianism on theological "decisionism," continuing hopes for "religious apocalypse," on anything but the atheistic fanaticism that denied all moral limits and culminated in the "self-enslavement" of man.

Manent on the Theological-Political Problem in Its Christian Form

If Mark Lilla upholds a much too narrow and dogmatic conception of the "Great Separation" between religion and politics, whose moderate tone conceals more radical and problematic assumptions, Pierre Manent's writ-

[5] Ibid., p. 298.

ings offer a rich, balanced, and suggestive rendering of the theological-political problem in its Western Christian form. Manent in no way disagrees with Lilla that the "Great Separation" forms the *starting point* for understanding liberty as liberty has been conceived and practiced for three centuries in the modern West.

But Manent appreciates, as Lilla does not, that the liberal West is the product of much more than the Great Separation. He *thinks* the accommodation that Ralph Hancock has so ably spoken of. A regime of consent depends upon a "body"—a political form such as the nation—that is an estimable inheritance from the West's predemocratic past. Western liberty in practice took shape from the fruitful coming together of the "neutral" liberal state and the *Christian* nation in a way that moderated the pretensions of early-modern political philosophy to begin the world anew. For Manent, the great human and political imperative is to tie together "communion" and "liberty" in a way that does justice to both. The historical achievement of the democratic nation was inseparable from its capacity to do this. In contrast, philosophical liberalism has next to nothing to say about the necessity and desirability of the political art of weaving community and liberty together. It also regularly fails to consider the Christian religion on its own terms.

Manent recognizes that Hobbes's architecture of separations played a crucial role in bringing civil peace to the West and in tracing the design of a *civil association* shorn of sectarian fanaticism. That is no mean achievement. As liberalized and democratized by his great successors such as Locke, Montesquieu, and Hume, the order of separations has allowed masses of human beings to live in relative peace and prosperity and has even found a real place for the goods of the soul—including religious freedom and affirmation—within civil society. But that is not the end of the story. Pierre Manent's work is particularly helpful in allowing us to see how the original separation must be mediated in practice and overcome in thought if the freedom and dignity of human beings is to be genuinely safeguarded.

As Manent writes in his 2006 book *La raison des nations: Réflexions sur la démocratie en Europe*, "If the separation of church and state is precious as a rule of our actions, it becomes ruinous if we make it the rule of our thought."[6] To make it the rule of our thought is to deny the directedness of the human mind toward truth, toward "the sovereignty of the object." It is to permanently sever liberty from a searching engagement with the ends or purposes of human freedom. Lilla's "art of intellectual separation," in a desperate effort to maintain civil peace, risks giving rise

[6] Pierre Manent, *La raison des nations: Réflexions sur la démocratie en Europe* (Paris: Galliment, 2006), p. 11.

to a new dogmatism that denies the natural movement of the human soul toward truth. It also assumes that the "theological-political problem" is frozen in time and ignores the new threats to human freedom that have arisen out of the modern "solution" to this problem. Those threats include the specters of soft and hard despotism, as well as indifference to truth. These can be summed up in the striking phrase of Aurel Kolnai: the "self-enslavement of man" that is a by-product of the most radical and consistent interpretations of human self-sovereignty.

Beyond the Modern "Solution"?

But to recognize the grave problems to which the modern "solution" to the West's theological-political problem has given rise is not to gainsay the necessity of something like a "liberal" solution to the West's theological-political problem. There were good reasons indeed for the "liberal" replacement of "authoritarian" religion, "whose dogmas and commandments were a part of political law,"[7] by a radically new emphasis on "rights" to freedom of religion or religious conscience. As Manent writes in his 1994 book *The City of Man*, "the early Moderns separated the law from the good because they had come to the conclusion that it was no longer possible for the ends of man to have a place in the law. Men had ideas about ends that were too incompatible; these disagreements easily degenerated; what mattered above all was to avoid civil war, which is the greatest of evils."[8]

Some liberals also emphasized, in a manner not incompatible with traditional moral philosophy, that truth and virtue must be freely sought and chosen. Manent points out that liberal-minded modern thinkers such as Milton (in his *Areopagitica*) and Lessing (in *The Education of the Human Race*) had high hopes that the pursuit of truth and goodness would flourish when they were freed from oppressive political and ecclesiastical control. There was indeed something noble about the affirmation of liberty as the essential precondition for the pursuit of virtue and truth and the concomitant recognition that liberty itself must never lose sight of human excellence. Yet Manent is not being unduly negative when he suggests that these high hopes have been sorely disappointed. There is need for new efforts for reviving these once noble liberal aspirations.

In *The City of Man*, Manent provides a particularly illuminating explanation for liberalism's drift toward militant indifference to truth. The *authorization* of every citizen to pursue his good in the private realm risks

[7] Pierre Manent, *The City of Man* (Princeton, N.J.: Princeton University Press, 1998), p. 179.

[8] Ibid.

becoming a new command or injunction to ignore the pursuit of truth and goodness in the name of respecting the equality of every human being's subjective judgment. The liberal order allows indifference "toward all goods that are the object of human searching, even truth, which is the chief good."[9] The spirit of radical modernity takes things a step further. The radical relativist *commands* indifference to the truth thus giving rise to a new and paradoxical order of "authoritarian command," this time in the name of a punishing relativism or political correctness. What began as a salutary effort to prevent the appropriation of the idea of the good by political and ecclesiastical tyrants becomes a new source of tyranny and dehumanization, the "dictatorship of relativism" famously spoken of by Pope Benedict XVI a few days before his selection as Pope in April of 2005.

This analysis is in no way put forward with antiliberal intent. But the preservation of the noble aspirations of liberalism demands resisting the full implementation of the project of intellectual separation, since that project ultimately demands the radical severing of human freedom from the moral contents of life. The law cannot be fully "neutral" about the good life—about the ends and purposes of human life—without eventually subverting the idea of human nobility and the moral foundations of liberty itself.

The Emancipation of the Will

In a remarkably synthetic 1993 essay entitled "Christianity and Democracy: Some Remarks on the Political History of Religion, or, on the Religious History of Modern Politics," Manent brilliantly highlights the dialectical twists and turns that have defined the relationship between religion and politics under conditions of modernity. In important respects, he argues, modernity can be understood as a self-conscious project committed to the "emancipation of the will" from any subordination to the dual requirements of nature and grace. This emancipation finds its most willful expressions in the theoretical and practical radicalism of Machiavelli and Nietzsche, two thinkers at the beginning and end of the modern movement who combined "the unlimited affirmation of the human will" with an "unlimited polemic against Christianity." Still, the success of our democracies serves to obscure "the extraordinary audacity of the original project of establishing the human world on the narrow point of the human will."[10]

---

[9] Ibid., p. 190.

[10] Pierre Manent, "Christianity and Democracy: Some Remarks on the Political History of Religion, or, on the Religious History of Modern Politics," in *Modern Liberty and Its Discontents*, ed. and trans. Daniel J. Mahoney and Paul Seaton (Lanham, Md.: Rowman and Littlefield, 1998), p. 101.

Manent points out that it was the Catholic Church that for the longest time insisted that liberalism (or naturalism, as she sometimes called it) would inevitably give way to more radical and consistent forms of human self-affirmation, such as socialism or communism. It is easy today to criticize the Church for her failure to appreciate the considerable benefits of the new liberal order. But for all her faults, the Church was properly sensitive to the "willfulness" inherent in the modern project. It was not wrong to discern totalitarian tendencies at work in modern democracy itself. As Manent points out it was the experience of "totalitarian democracy" in both its Jacobin and Bolshevik forms that led to a specifically *liberal* discovery—or rediscovery—of religion and to a more robust Christian or Catholic defense of constitutionalism and human rights.[11] Conservative-minded liberals and antitotalitarian Christians were henceforth united by a rejection of human self-sovereignty. They came to appreciate that the "regulated will," one that deferred to God and the law, and not one emancipated from natural and moral restraints, is the hallmark of a genuinely free and humane social order.

Constant and Tocqueville: The Liberal Rediscovery of Religion

Manent cites the example of Benjamin Constant as an exemplar of this paradoxical reconciliation between Christianity and liberalism. The Swiss-born Constant was a Huguenot and anticleric who had no sympathies for the old regime or the political power of the Catholic Church. Yet he was appalled by the antireligious terrorism that accompanied the French Revolution and defended the rights and integrity of ordinary Catholic believers. Moreover, he saw in the terrible work of the French Revolutionary Convention the *effectual truth* of modern doctrines of sovereignty: the terror that flowed from making willfulness—no matter from where it originated, whether from the one, the few, or the many—the foundation of collective life. As Constant famously put it in the opening chapter of the *Principles of Politics Applicable to All Governments*, "[T]here are things too heavy for human hands."[12] Constant did not abandon the idea of the general will altogether since, properly interpreted, it was a way of combining majority rule with good government and the common good. But he rejected the "false metaphysics" that confused human liberty with the unfettered will of the people. In his political writings, he took aim at the confusion of the

[11] Ibid., pp. 103–4.

[12] Benjamin Constant, *Principles of Politics Applicable to All Governments*, ed. Etienne Hofman, trans. Dennis O'Keefe (Indianapolis, Ind.: Liberty Fund, 2003), p. 20.

popular sources of authority with a guarantee of justice and the general good. He set out to rescue liberalism from that revolutionary inebriation that refused to bow before sacred limits or restraints. He never stopped repeating that "there is a part of human existence which remains individual and independent, and by right beyond all political jurisdiction." Confronting the first manifestations of "totalitarian democracy," Constant broke with the official ideology of the French Revolution and affirmed that "sovereignty exists only in a limited or relative way."[13]

Like Burke or the French counterrevolutionaries such as Joseph de Maistre, Constant criticized the pretensions of modern philosophy and affirmed a spiritual realm or space above the human will. Unlike the conservative or reactionary critics of the French Revolution, however, he used this insight at the service of a chastened liberalism. However, one must note that he never defines the ultimate source of these limits upon the human will. He evokes religion as a reminder of the sublime and a symbol of the ineffable, as the source of generous feelings and noble action, and as a consolation amidst misery. He sympathized with religion without being particularly religious and had none of Tocqueville's (qualified) sympathies for traditional faith. He is finally more clear about what he rejects—absolute sovereignty or unlimited willfulness—than he is about what he affirms. Constant is the first modern thinker to limn a "negative" argument for an order of things above the human will. Like many twentieth-century antitotalitarian thinkers, he is too much of a modern man to simply believe in the old verities and far too decent—and reflective—to dispense with them altogether.

As Manent argues, conservative-minded liberals such as Constant and Tocqueville found for religion "its specifically modern moral political and moral credibility." They praised it "for the very reason it was formerly and even recently criticized: it is something *above* the human will."[14] Constant saw that religion kept human beings in mind of the noble and the beautiful, and of those obligations that transcend the will of men. For his part, Tocqueville deplored a "pantheism" that conflated the divine and human and that weakened moral agency by making human beings playthings of vast cosmological, historical, and sociological forces. He, too, deplored absolute and unlimited human sovereignty and attacked the "impious maxim" that "in the interest of society all is permitted."[15] As Manent helpfully puts it, for Tocqueville religion could moderate the effects of both the

---

13 Ibid., p. 31.

14 Pierre Manent, "Christianity and Democracy," p. 104.

15 Ibid., p. 106.

"new activism" (such as "tyranny of the majority") and the "new passivity" (democratic man's tendency to succumb to apathetic withdrawal and engrossment in everyday life) to which democracy gave rise.[16] As Tocqueville famously argues in the opening chapters of the second volume of *Democracy in America*, democratic theorists proclaim that human beings should take their bearings only from their own lights, that they should disregard the authority of tradition or anything that is not discernable by the light of reason. But human beings need authoritative beliefs or "dogmas" to live well. Without the moral maxims provided by religion they are likely to succumb to a psychological and spiritual "vertigo" that gives way either to nihilism or to conformism with all its illiberal political consequences.

The conclusion is clear: liberty must in decisive respects be "liberty under God" if it is to do justice to the spiritual nature and limitations of human beings. Liberty understood as pure indetermination does not allow human beings to avoid the twin temptations of democratic tyranny and the listlessness born of exaggerating our capacity to make our way in the world unguided by the spiritual or philosophical inheritance of the past. And listlessness leads to despotism. Of such thoughts, Lilla seems to have no inkling.

The Church and Liberal Democracy: What Kind of Accommodation?

Our analysis has stressed the vulnerability of philosophical liberalism to subversion from within. Various forms of "hard" and "soft" self-sovereignty (I owe this helpful distinction to Jean Bethke Elshtain)[17] threaten to erode the moral foundations of democracy. If the temptation of a certain kind of decayed liberalism is to identify "choice" or "consent" with willful self-assertion (in the seemingly more "liberal" and benign form of support for abortion on demand, cloning, and various forms of biotechnological "enhancement"), the temptation of conservatives (or conservative-minded liberals) is to think that the problem that self-sovereignty poses for modern democracy can be rhetorically defined out of existence. For the conservative-minded, this takes the form of "baptizing" liberal democracy in a way that obscures its connections to the modern enlightenment project. This is the temptation that the post-Vatican II Catholic Church has not always successfully resisted. A series of prominent twentieth-century

[16] Ibid.

[17] See Jean Bethke Elshtain, *Sovereignty: God, State and Self* (New York: Basic Books, 2008), especially the chapter entitled "Self-Sovereignty: Moralism, Nihilism, and Existential Isolation."

Catholic thinkers from the French Thomist philosopher Jacques Maritain to Pope John Paul II have located the origins of equality and the "rights of man" in the teachings of the Gospels themselves. They have been too eager to argue for the essential compatibility of Christianity and democracy rather than putting the stress on the need for a fulsome prudential accommodation between the Church and the liberal order. For all its practical merits, this "Christian Democratic" position obscures the origins of philosophical liberalism in a polemical reaction to the political power of the Church. It also ignores the insight of an older, more "anti-modern" Church that the "rights of man" were too often claimed at the expense of the "rights of God."[18]

Instead of proclaiming the Christian origins of liberalism, or confusing Christianity with secular humanitarianism as progressivist Christians are prone to do, the Church can contribute to the cause of freedom by upholding the truth as it understands it. When Pope Benedict XVI warned in his September 2006 Regensburg lecture against reducing Christianity to a "humanitarian moral message" he was speaking both in the name of the integrity of the faith and out of genuine solicitude for the well-being of a liberal or democratic order.[19] Christianity can exercise its influence on the

---

[18] Pope John Paul II paid his respects to this older understanding when he acknowledged in 1991 that all those who are "convinced that they know the truth, and firmly adhere to it, are considered unreliable from a democratic point of view" (see p. 17). But in his contribution to this volume, Cardinal George draws a somewhat questionable conclusion from this perfectly legitimate insight. His article suggests a more fundamental opposition between Catholicism and the American proposition than is warranted by the historical record or the self-understanding of the American republic. My suggestion is that it is both imprudent and unnecessary to identify America as a liberal republic with the hostility of the "world" to the truth of the Gospel. To do justice to both the integrity of the faith and the requirements of moral and political prudence (that cardinal virtue which, in Burke's famous words, can be seen as the "god of this world below") obliges Christians to refuse the twin extremes of "kneeling before the world" (Maritain) and "despising the temporal" (Charles Péguy). To identify American democracy with the "world" as such comes perilously close to "despising the world." It is one thing to criticize the excesses of "American culture," as Cardinal George rightly does; it is another thing to identify them with our regime principles as such. A more balanced approach might acknowledge the self-radicalizing tendencies in democratic culture while highlighting the fact that the American civic tradition contains ample resources for opposing the identification of liberty with soft nihilism or radical autonomy. In my view, Catholics are no more obliged to be critics of the American proposition than to be proponents of an untenable *theoretical* reconciliation between Christianity and democracy.

[19] Pope Benedict XVI, "Faith, Reason and the University: Memories and Reflections" (lecture, University of Regensburg, Germany, September 12, 2006), sec. 38.

souls of men, it can help fortify an understanding of liberty as "liberty under God," only if it rejects the temptation to become a wholly "democratic" religion. The Church does not serve the cause of human liberty; she cannot play its part in overcoming the democratic "activism" and "passivity" so feared by Tocqueville, unless it stands for something more substantial than a commitment to humanitarian "values" and egalitarian "social justice." Nor do persistent demands for the internal "democratization" of the churches contribute to their ability to remind democratic men and women of the ultimate dependence of liberty upon truth. The churches would then bow to consent as their governing principle. We have arrived at what we might call the Tocquevillian conundrum or problematic: liberal democracy needs the wisdom, self-restraint, and elevation provided by religion, but over time democracy tends to "democratize" all the contents of life, including religion itself. As thinly disguised humanitarianism, as a project to promote this-worldly transformation, religion ceases to be "something above the human will."

Toward a Chastened Liberalism

Careful reflection on this problem serves to moderate any excessive hopes for creating a new postliberal consensus that could purge liberalism of its intrinsic—and historical—identification with human self-sovereignty. The nineteenth-century American Catholic journalist, writer, and political philosopher Orestes Brownson perfectly captured the nature of this conundrum in his 1865 work *The American Republic.*[20] Brownson noted that the "state of nature" doctrine—the idea that government arises from a compact or contract among equal, independent, and sovereign individuals—was part of the "political tradition" of the United States. In the famous words of the Declaration of Independence, government "derives its just powers from the consent of the governed." All Americans—one might add almost everyone in the liberal West today—agree that no man has the right to govern another human being without his consent. But some locate this prohibition against despotic rule in the absolute freedom or "autonomy" of the individual, while others, including many of the Founders themselves, denied that the individual has a "sovereign right even to himself, or the right to dispose of himself as he pleases." The same doctrine is thus remarkably equivocal: it can be understood in light of the requirements of either autonomy, on the one hand, or in light of a more traditional understanding of "liberty under God" on the other. In this

[20] See Orestes A. Brownson, *The American Republic*, introduction by Peter Augustine Lawler (Wilmington, Del.: ISI Books, 2003).

equivocation or indetermination one can find the deepest roots of the "culture wars" that have raged in the United States (and to some extent in other Western democracies) in recent decades.

We are left with a choice: we can conceive man as sovereign lord of existence, the autonomous creator of his own "values," or we can see in him a being who participates in a natural order that he did not make, an "order of things" that gives meaning to his freedom and that makes sense of his search for truth. In the latter understanding, eloquently upheld by Brownson, "man is not God, independent, self-existing, and self-sufficing." Rather, "he is dependent, and dependent not only on his Maker, but on his fellow-men, on society, and even on nature, or the material world."[21] The task of a chastened liberalism, no less than of a Christian religion faithful to its own wisdom, is to remind men and women inebriated with the ideology of consent that human beings are truly free only when they know they are not gods. The next task is to draw the appropriate moral and political conclusions from this insight.

---

[21] Ibid., p. 39.

CHAPTER 5

Taking Catholicism and Democracy Seriously

MARC D. GUERRA
Ave Maria University

THE RELATIONSHIP between organized religion and civil society is the subject of ardent, sometimes heated debate within the Western democracies. The most immediate and visible reason for this is the spectacular and horrifying terrorist attacks of September 11, 2001. Such an event was not wholly unforeseen. Eight years earlier, Harvard professor Samuel Huntington published a widely debated and provocative article in *Foreign Affairs* titled "The Clash of Civilizations?" Huntington argued that with the collapse of the Soviet Union the West now faced a different geopolitical challenge. That challenge included the possibility of a looming, open confrontation with the militant brand of Islam that had taken hold in the Middle East over the previous two decades. Weeks after September 11, the term "clash of civilizations" had become part of the West's working vocabulary.

But the rise of radical Islam and its affiliated terrorist groups in the Middle East is not solely responsible for the West's renewed interest in what Spinoza called the theologico-political problem.

There are homegrown reasons as well. Under the leadership of former French president d'Estaing, for example, the Convention on the Future of Europe hotly debated whether Christianity's historic role in shaping European civilization merited any mention in the European Union's first constitution. Representatives from France, Spain, and the Netherlands argued that the European Union constitution should not include any reference to God whatsoever. Closer to home, since the 1980s vocal and visible members of America's political class and punditry have warned about the purported dangers of the so-called Religious Right in American politics.

Political arguments over the legal status of abortion on demand and "same-sex marriage" are popularly portrayed as examples of the ongoing "culture wars" between "conservative Christians" and "secular" defenders of civil liberties. In the 2008 Republican presidential primaries, we witnessed an at-times nasty debate among Evangelical Christians as to whether a Mormon should be elected to the presidency.

The theologico-political problem is not new. It is as old as Western political thought itself. The unnamed Athenian Stranger in Plato's *Laws* opens that dialogue by abruptly asking two aged citizens, "Is it a god or some human being, strangers, who is given the credit for laying down your laws?"[1] That we are apt to think that this problem is relatively new is largely the result of the kind of regime in which we live. Seeking to find a political solution to the bloody religious wars that engulfed Europe after the Reformation, early modern philosophers such as Hobbes, Locke, and Spinoza unleashed new forms of rationalism and republicanism that were designed to solve the problem of the relation between God and politics. In contrast to the classical political philosophers, they self-consciously sought to align wisdom with political power through the project of universal enlightenment. This new state of affairs necessitated a reversal of the classical understanding of the proper relation of virtue or human excellence to political life. Political life no longer would be seen to exist for the sake of moral and intellectual virtue, what Aristotle felicitously referred to as the good life. Henceforth, virtue would be subordinated to securing those goods necessary for man's material and physical well-being within political society.

Denying the political utility of reflections on the summum bonum, or man's final end, the Enlightenment philosophers proposed a regime that did not adjudicate between the myriad of spiritual goods that arise within political life. The goal of the modern regime would be far less lofty. It would limit itself to providing for man's bodily needs and securing his newly discovered fundamental right to freedom. Ostensibly liberating man from all natural and divine restraints, modern political philosophy would transform the theologico-political question into a technical problem. In other words, liberal democracy was first presented by its philosophic exponents as the solution to the problem of religiously disrupted politics. By harmonizing the tensions between reason, morality, and God, the modern liberal state would settle the problem of God and politics once and for all. The gradual acceptance of this bold claim, more than any

---

[1] Plato, *The Laws*, trans. Thomas L. Pangle (Chicago: University of Chicago Press, 1980), p. 624a.

other reason, explains why many citizens in democratic states today believe that the reemergence of the theologico-political problem represents something new under the sun.

An increasingly common—though ultimately muddled—response to this problem is to insist that citizens and statesmen reaffirm their commitment to philosophic liberalism's original separation of religion and politics. This thesis has most recently been advanced by Mark Lilla in his engaging, if finally flawed, *The Stillborn God*.[2] Lilla argues that the "Great Separation" that Hobbes and his followers effected, which severed modern politics of ties to any explicit cosmological and theological claim, is now imperiled. Tracing the intellectual, religious, and political course of this separation, Lilla discovers that the Great Separation suffered its first internal crisis less than a century after Hobbes's death. Although he agreed with Hobbes about the undesirability of theological politics, Rousseau attempted to channel man's naturally religious impulses into the service of civil society. This ill-conceived tactic would be taken up and modified, in different ways, by Kant and Hegel, culminating in the latter's claim that a quasi-religious conviction formed the fecund core of a people's national identity. One of the tragic effects of that claim, according to Lilla, was that it left liberal Protestantism ripe for political exploitation (as it was in World War I) and open to embracing atavistic, messianic politics (as it was in World War II).

Over and against this sad state of affairs, Lilla seeks to remind us that "we are heirs of the Great Separation only if we wish to be."[3] But if we still wish to be, we must now recommit ourselves to the bold proposition behind that separation. As Lilla breathlessly concludes, we must be publicly willing to admit that "it is wiser to beware the forces unleashed by the Bible's messianic promise than to try exploiting them for public good."[4] More than anything else, this conviction explains why "we have chosen to keep our politics unilluminated by the light of revelation" and instead are solely reliant upon "our own lucidity."[5]

Setting aside the accuracy and adequacy of Lilla's genealogy of the theologico-political problem, one cannot help but be struck by the incredible serenity with which he states his conclusion. John Courtney Murray, S.J., acknowledged that "today [1960] . . . the serene, and often naïve, certainties

[2] Mark Lilla, *The Stillborn God: Religion, Politics, and the Modern West* (New York: Alfred A. Knopf, 2007).

[3] Ibid., p. 306.

[4] Ibid., p. 308.

[5] Ibid.

of the eighteenth century have crumbled."[6] As a result, the self-evidence of those truths that were once believed to undergird our modern democratic institutions now "may legitimately be questioned." Murray had the moral and intellectual courage to admit that no intellectually honest man could defend either the goodness or desirability of modern democracy simply on philosophic liberalism's original premises. Thus Murray set out to show that America's Founders "built better than they knew." Truthful recognition of the radical limits of Enlightenment rationalism requires the contemporary defender of what is genuinely good and desirable about modern democracy to root that defense in an argument that does not require "a basic betrayal of the existential structure of reality itself."[7] Viewed in this light, Lilla's plea that we must recommit ourselves to the original proposition behind the Great Separation seems far too complacent, if not outright naïve.

For these reasons, it is remarkable to observe that the moral and spiritual demands of Christian faith today are routinely seen to require the political affirmation of equality and freedom that is only found in liberal democracies. Jean-Marie Cardinal Lustiger, for example, remarked, arrestingly, that "it has been more and more widely recognized that liberty, equality, and fraternity are among the fruits borne by the Biblical and Christian tradition."[8] This is not a new development, though. The belief that modern democracy has its roots in Christianity first gained prominence in the early part of the nineteenth century. The spirit of this argument was famously captured by Chateaubriand, who declared in *The Genius of Christianity* (1802) that the arrangements of the modern world had their origins in the structures of medieval Christendom. A similar chord was struck by Lord Acton, who in a moment of enthusiasm declared that the works of Aquinas contain "the earliest exposition of the Whig theory of the revolution."[9] This thesis would be reworked and presented in different ways in the writings of various authors, from the non-Christian Hegel to the unmistakably anti-Christian Nietzsche. In the twentieth century, however, the so-called secularization thesis would undergo a modification in the hands of Christian thinkers, who began to

---

[6] John Courtney Murray, S.J., *We Hold These Truths: Catholic Reflections on the American Proposition* (1960; repr., Kansas City, Kans.: Sheed and Ward, 1988), p. viii. Page references are to the 1988 edition.

[7] Ibid., p. 310.

[8] Jean-Marie Cardinal Lustiger, "Liberty, Equality, and Fraternity," in *First Things* 76 (October, 1997): 39.

[9] Lord Acton, "The History of Freedom in Christianity," in *Essays in the History of Liberty* (Indianapolis, Ind.: Liberty Fund, 1985), p. 34.

argue that not only was their religion compatible with the modern regime but that it received its best political articulation in democracy.

The belief that Christian faith is compatible with only one type of political regime, namely, modern liberal democracy, is something new. In fact, it flies in the face of Catholic thought's long and rich tradition of theologico-political reflection. Routinely oscillating between its Augustinian and Thomistic poles, that tradition consistently emphasizes the fundamentally transpolitical nature of the Christian faith. Catholic theologico-political reflection received its first, and in my judgment unsurpassed, articulation in Augustine's *The City of God.* That work dialectically examines the great claimants that vie for the loyalty of men's souls and, in so doing, articulates the essential moral and theological structure of the Christian community's relation to the city. Augustine's trenchant argument outlines the traditional warp and woof of Catholic theologico-political reflection through its famous discussion of two different but in some ways related cities, the City of God and the earthly city.

According to Augustine, these two cities have their respective origins in two different loves. The heavenly City, or the City of God, refers to that spiritual association binding those whose love is rightly ordered to God. While the term is most appropriately used to refer to the community of saints and angels that gaze upon God's essence in the beatific vision, Augustine also uses it to describe the visible and invisible living community of Christian faithful who, from the time of Abel, have participated in the life of the heavenly City through the outpouring of God's grace. By contrast, the earthly city is animated by a love of creation rather than the Creator, by a love of the self rather than a love of God. Tracing its origins back to Cain's fratricide of Abel, the earthly city to some degree historically overlaps with the City of God. And yet despite this historical intermingling, the ethos of the earthly city distinguishes it from the providentially achieved spiritual perfection of the City of God.

Political life as we know it, in Augustine's account, came into existence as a result of the Fall. Due to man's primordial act of proud disobedience to God, political rule is necessary primarily in order to help coercively control, or at least to lessen, the effects of man's sinful nature in the world. The earthly city does not seek to uphold perfect justice, but rather the more limited and modest goal of establishing some recognizable form of temporal peace. The theologico-political challenge facing the Christian community is to find a prudential way in which the lofty demands placed upon man by the Gospel can be accommodated to the limited but still necessary demands of the political order. Responding to this challenge, Augustine thus set before himself a task not entirely different from the one that Plato's

Socrates undertakes in the *Republic*: to give an account of why a man who has come to understand his life in terms of something beyond the political willingly should reattach himself to the life of the city. Augustine's response to this challenge was to argue that the moral teachings of Christian faith require men to look on their political obligations as a religious duty. Christianity's injunction to love one's neighbor as himself—the exact opposite of the antisocial and antipolitical stance that the ancient city claimed the classical philosophers struck—did not mean that Christians should slight their responsibilities within civil society. Instead, the theological virtue of charity demanded that Christians were obliged to devote themselves to the good of their fellow citizens with an intensity that was unknown and unimaginable in the Greek polis. Emblematic of this new state of affairs is that while the philosopher in Plato's *Republic* memorably has to be forced to rule, Augustine argues that the Christian ought to "undertake righteous engagement" in human affairs out of the "compulsion of love."[10]

While Augustine explicitly rooted the Christian's participation in political life in the theological virtue of charity, the cornerstone of Aquinas's political thought is the Aristotelian notion of nature. Following Aristotle, Aquinas claimed that man is by nature "a social and political animal," who is naturally inclined to live within political society.[11] In the first instance, human beings are the most social and political of all animals precisely because they are also the most physically needy. It is this fact that initially inclines man to live in society. By nature, the first society that man belongs to is the family or the household. However, the specific good of the family is at best only a partial good, since its principal and most immediate aim is the procurement of those things that allow for and sustain human life. Ruled by economics or the art of household management, the family cannot secure all the goods that human beings need to survive, much less flourish. Aquinas saw the family as being completed by political society. As the most perfect natural association, the political community incorporates and comprehends all lesser communities and regulates them to its own end.

The natural primacy of the city is connected with other, higher aspects of human nature. Because man is a rational animal, it is not sufficient that he merely "lives, but that he lives well."[12] Indeed, as Aquinas states in his discussion of natural law, the highest and most distinctively human of man's natural inclinations prompts him to know the truth and

---

10 St. Augustine, *The City of God* 19.19.

11 St. Thomas Aquinas, *On Kingship* 1.4.

12 St. Thomas Aquinas, *Commentary on Aristotle's Nicomachean Ethics* 1.1.4.

to live virtuously within society. Aquinas believed that such flourishing best occurs in the political community, the most perfect of all human societies. In contrast to the household, which exists for the sake of procreation and the education of offspring, the political community *is* able to achieve a level of self-sufficiency. It ultimately exists for the sake of the good life, the life of moral and intellectual virtue. Cultivated through participation in such distinctively political actions as ruling and being ruled in turn, the good of the political community is "common" to all citizens. The virtuous habits instilled in those citizens who live under well-ordered polities—a crucial point that for Aquinas takes on great significance given Christianity's inherently transpolitical nature—help to perfect man's nature. The common good thus constitutes the "proper" good of the citizen. Aquinas clearly understood the kind of natural perfection that can occur in political life to be inferior to the supernatural perfection that can only come about through the reception of God's grace. But he did not believe that man's spiritual perfection negated his natural perfection. Aquinas understood, in other words, that only the man who is "depraved, a beast as it were," or the man who is "better than a man, a god as it were," is capable of living outside of civil society.[13]

Today serious reflection on the two poles of Christian citizenship can help us take the measure of modern democracy's characteristic strengths and weaknesses, of its distinctive virtues and vices. Modern democracy powerfully affirms the fundamental legitimacy and desirability of undeniable social and political goods such as civic peace, religious freedom, self-government, and constitutionalism. At the same time, philosophic liberalism, the theory behind modern democracy, gradually erodes the moral, political, and spiritual life of the regime it helped bring into existence. For it typically champions a view of freedom that weakens its citizens' basic attachment to those inherited extra democratic goods like religion and morality that liberal democracy must rely upon for its health and survival. Currently that understanding of freedom is routinely identified with a radical view of human autonomy. Consequently, contemporary democracy tends to be both egalitarian and leveling. As such, it not only abhors all natural and moral limits but increasingly those political limits placed on men by liberal democracy itself. Catholic political thought can help present-day democrats—Christian and non-Christian—rediscover the necessity, desirability, and nobility of humanizing limits.

But in pursuing this rediscovery, Catholic political thought must resist the temptation to ape modernity and formulate its own "solution" to the

[13] St. Thomas Aquinas, *Commentary on Aristotle's Politics* 1.1.39.

theologico-political problem. It must find a *prudent* way of coming to terms with democracy's discontents and modern philosophy's disenchantment of the world. Weber famously traced the roots of this moral and spiritual disenchantment to modern science and its unprecedented success in systematically exorcising any sense of meaning or mystery in man's world. The disenchantment of the world is a reality we experience daily, an inescapable fact seared into our all too modern consciousness. In light of Nietzsche's "annihilating critique" of the "last men" who naïvely believed they "had discovered happiness," Weber somberly concluded there was no intellectually honest way for late modern man to think that reason could discover any vital sense of meaning or value in the world.[14] As Weber jeeringly remarked, who "believes in this?—aside from a few big children in university chairs and editorial offices."

But in responding to modernity's discontents, Catholic moral and political thought should not attempt to transform or merely transcend modernity. Instead, it must proceed prudently, attempting to retain the authentic social, political, and scientific gains that modernity has helped bring about. In this way it does justice to the full truth about man and the nature of reality. Such thought can rightly be called postmodern conservatism. Catholic political thought can defend what is genuinely good in the present because it is able to view the present from a perspective outside of modernity. From this untimely and enlarged perspective, Catholic political thought can, for example, acknowledge the compelling truth in modern democracy's conception of justice and its affirmation of the nobility of self-rule. At the same time, it can remind liberal democracy of the natural inequalities and hierarchies that exist among real human beings and thus affirm the virtues of both aristocracy and democracy. By so doing, it calls critical attention to the ongoing need—and possibilities—for both kinds of virtue within contemporary civil societies.

Catholic political thought has a healthy critical edge as well. It seeks to expose the dehumanizing consequences of modern rationalism's claim of nature's basic indifference to the moral, intellectual, and spiritual ends that animate human beings and philosophic liberalism's reduction of real men and women to abstract individuals. It puts contemporary man in a position to see through modern rationalism's Sisyphean attempt to construct a world that would dissolve the antinomies that mark a genuinely human life. Moreover, it would help him to appreciate the myriad of goods that he has been given by nature. That appreciation provides inti-

[14] Max Weber, "Science as a Vocation," *Max Weber: Sociological Writings*, ed. Wolf Heydebrand (New York: Continuum, 1994), p. 290.

mations that despite all that nature has given us and all we do for ourselves we remain somewhat alienated. We have reason to believe that our true home lies elsewhere, that it is in our nature to long for a personal God. Indeed, the recognition of this truth is a defining characteristic of Catholic political thought.

To acknowledge the alienated character of human life is in part to recognize the grounds of Christianity's distinctive teaching on the greatness and misery of man. Christianity, Pascal pointedly observed, "is strange." Christianity tells man he is a fallen and wretched creature, and it also tells him he is an alien in this world and bids him to live a life that imitates Christ's. Yet by affirming the moral and spiritual paradox that is man, Christianity saves man from himself by calling him into communion with God. Pascal saw only too well that unless the greatness and misery of man are recognized, men inevitably become either horribly vain or horribly abject. The perceived strangeness of Christian realism mirrors and therefore partially explains the strangeness of human beings themselves.

Christianity's realistic appreciation of fallen man's qualified alienation stands in sharp contrast to the disquieting moral and spiritual isolation that mark the real life of liberalism's great abstraction: the rights-bearing modern individual. Truth be told, the free and equal individuals which philosophic liberalism describes do not exist by nature. By denying the existence of all natural or divine restraints placed on man and asserting that he is essentially an asocial being, liberalism, however, theoretically allowed for the emergence of this new human type. And the course of modern democracy has increasingly produced instances of this type. As Pierre Manent has felicitously observed, modern democratic life requires man to engage "in an exploration of what it means to *become* an individual."[15]

To the extent that democratic man thinks of himself as an individual, he believes that he is free from all familial, social, political, and religious ties. The idea of the rights-bearing individual has had remarkable success in changing the way in which men view themselves and the world. Under this idea, all human actions are prone to be interpreted as matters of consent. The individual is thought to be the sole source of legitimacy. To cite Manent again, "anything which is added to the individual . . . is only a more or less regrettable necessity, and not something that has any real human *meaning*."[16] This view undoubtedly feeds into the propensity of democratic citizens to feel a sense of detachment from the political societies

---

15 Pierre Manent, "On Modern Individualism," *Modern Liberty and Its Discontents*, ed. and trans. Daniel J. Mahoney and Paul Seaton (Lanham, Md.: Rowman and Littlefield, 1998), p. 152 (italics added).

16 Ibid., p. 155.

in which they live. It also helps explain why democratic citizens are prone to view the common good not as the "weal" the political community justly holds in common but merely as the sum total of material and economic goods to which all citizens legally ought to have access. But its effects are not limited merely to the political order. It can, for example, be seen in the increased tendency in the West today to understand marriage not as a natural society that grows out of the desire of men and women to couple and procreate but as a partnership forged by consenting adults seeking mutual self-fulfillment. And it also helps explain why legislators within liberal democracies currently find it difficult to formulate any reasoned, nonscriptural based objection to the democratic individual's asserted right to same-sex marriage. What is more, it fuels the claims of those who argue that the hierarchical Catholic Church should be "democratically" reorganized and that Church doctrine—especially on moral matters—should be grounded in the consent of "the people of God."

Individualism erodes human beings' understanding of themselves as social and political beings and flattens their understanding of the mystery of the human soul. Today, the rights-bearing individual is believed to be able to construct his own happiness through self-realization and self-determination. Belief in such creative abilities weakens one's sense of indebtedness to family, friends, country, and God. It insidiously isolates the individual from other human beings and ultimately from himself. Contrary to the uneasy but partially satisfied alienation of which Christianity speaks, individualism cultivates an outwardly liberating but inwardly crippling sense of sovereignty.

Despite the palpable effects of this form of thinking, the real men and women that live in liberal democracies remain much more than mere modern individuals. While they may think of themselves as individuals, they nonetheless live—and also think of themselves—as daughters, husbands, friends, citizens, and men of faith. To greater or lesser degrees, they still live as naturally social, political, and religious human beings. Yet given liberal democracy's tendency to foster a view of the artificial or constructed character of human life, men currently find it difficult to understand, let alone explain, the meaning of the kind of lives they naturally desire to live. For this reason, Catholic political thought must defend and help cultivate the moral foundations of democracy.

Among other things, those foundations are today eroded by the idea of human dignity and autonomy. Prevailing theories of human dignity tend to be a vulgarized version of Kant's moral teaching. The upholding of a truly rational—hence universal—morality, which for Kant was the ultimate expression of human dignity, hinged upon postulating the existence of God, freedom, and immortality. However, most contemporary theories of human dignity only see the necessity of postulating the existence of human autonomy. In so doing, they not only strip morality of the rigorous demands Kant placed on it but also infuse the idea of human autonomy with even more significance than it had in Kant's moral system. Emptied of content as well as criteria, it bears the entire burden of moral and political life and thought. Human dignity is seen to require the exercise of human autonomy, and the exercise of human autonomy is seen to be definitive proof of human dignity. In short, a perfect circle is formed.

One important way to counter the corrosive moral and political effects of this understanding of human dignity is to remind democratic citizens and statesmen that liberal democracy relies on the moral structure of human freedom for its health and survival. Given its powerful affirmation of such things as the moral equality of all persons, the justice and nobility of self-rule, and the indispensability of constitutional law, modern democracy is rich with moral content. And yet the very logic of philosophic liberalism's deracinated view of nature in general and human nature in particular defines that content in a remarkably formal or tautological way. Apologists for liberal democracies speak endlessly about the institutional and procedural requirements of human rights and self-governance yet remain conspicuously silent about how these things comport with, let alone ennoble, the nature of man and political life.

Over and against the typically modern desire for emancipation, citizens and statesmen in liberal democracies urgently need to recover an appreciation of "the basic truth that *response*, not *fiat*, is the prime gesture of the human person."[17] Central to this appreciation is the recognition that human beings participate in a hierarchical natural order that they themselves do not make. That recognition carries with it the affirmation of the humanizing limits placed on men as creatures—the exact opposite of the claim by the religion of humanity or the cult of the unencumbered self that man is or can be the omnipotent creator of all things, including himself. Without the positive affirmation of a metaphysical and natural order that grounds, shapes, and orients the exercise of human freedom, the very notions of equality and liberty to which democracy rightly gives political expression become unintelligible and indefensible. Indeed, only if political liberty is rooted in and reflective of a naturally given moral order is it able to ennoble the life of the citizen who exercises that freedom.

This picture of the structure of human freedom complements John Paul's argument in *The Splendor of the Truth*. That work emphasizes that

[17] Aurel Kolnai, "Privilege and Liberty," *Privilege and Liberty and Other Essays in Political Philosophy*, ed. Daniel J. Mahoney (Lanham, Md.: Lexington Books, 1999), p. 26.

human beings possess neither the freedom nor the power to determine the nature of good and evil. Rather, they have been given the ability to reason and act in accordance with a created moral order that is tethered to and informed by transcendent truth. Human freedom is therefore not an end in itself but a qualified good. It needs to be directed by natural and divine law if it is justly to be put in service of the truth about God and by extension the truth about man. As John Paul forcefully argues, when ordered to truth, the exercise of human freedom contributes to the perfection of man as man.

In addressing such salutary arguments to modern democracies, Catholic thinkers must not forget that by its very nature liberal democracy seeks to pit the rights of the sovereign individual against democracy's political need of an ordered liberty under God. Their task is Sisyphean. They must not forget this. In other words, they must think *politically*. They must not fall prey to the naïve belief that the mere presentation and acceptance of a theoretical argument can solve the problem of liberal democracy once and for all. To do so would replicate modern political philosophy's error: the belief that political life can be founded on and guided by "pure reason." Like the "umpire" of Aristotelian political philosophy, Catholic political thinkers must seek to moderate the modern regime from the inside, prudently working to curb, but not expecting to eradicate, its tendencies and excesses. Advancing the kind of "education relative to the regime"[18] that Aristotle points out is constantly necessary in political life, Catholic political thinkers should seek to counter modern democracy's dominant tendencies. They should remind citizens of liberal democracies that the ever-expanding proclamation of the demands of human rights needs to be moderated by a firm and steady recognition of the moral, political, and spiritual requirements of natural law.

From its inception, philosophic liberalism has tended to dissolve political life into the subpolitical realms of the "individual" and "society." More deeply, it affirmed two natural realities, the individual and humanity. Other groupings, including the political community, were based on consent. But today the persistent emphasis on the demands of universal human rights "has an incontestably anti-political flavor."[19] As Manent has recently shown, the idea of a "united humanity" configured around the recognition of human rights—an aspiration anticipated by Kant's moral dream of a truly cosmopolitan humanity—increasingly captivates the late modern Western mind. Such an idea gains support from Western man's

---

[18] Aristotle, *Politics* 5.9.

[19] Pierre Manent, *A World Beyond Politics? A Defense of the Nation-State*, trans. Marc Lepain (Princeton, N.J.: Princeton University Press, 2006), p. 99.

memory of the brutal totalitarian tyrannies of the twentieth century and his current fears of the escalating violence that would accompany a clash of civilizations. Administered by transnational courts and legal bureaucracies, such a world would pursue the material and moral well-being of man universally and abstractly conceived. The desire for such a world can be seen in the dominant idea of a united Europe. It also can be seen in the establishment of the international human rights court at the Hague and the growing belief among many in the West that the United Nations alone can sanction and administer the just use of military force.

The tension between what Manent describes as the "natural order of politics and the project and hope of a new metapolitical or postpolitical order"[20] reflects modern man's desire to seek refuge in abstractions like the "individual" or "humanity" that transcend the limiting, but for that reason humanizing, constraints of nature and political life. To a great degree, the dream of a world organized around the universal recognition of "the rights of man" is the logical conclusion of modern political philosophy's teaching on the individual in the state of nature. The individual as individual has no natural ties to a particular family, people, and, above all, to any particular political community. Formally, he exists in an abstract world inhabited by other rights-bearing individuals. Understood as such, he should be able to be affirmed abstractly, in other words, unfettered by the particular (hence limiting) claims of any genuinely *political* body or authority. Drawn to its logical conclusion and taken on its own terms, this means the notion of *human being* ought to be preferred to that of the *citizen*. This partially explains the growing tendency to reject the collective restraint linked to citizenship.

Late modernity's humanitarian desire to flee from the concrete, limiting realities of citizenship and political life can have its Christian analogue. Today, this typically takes the form of giving undue or inappropriate social and political emphasis to an eschatologically conceived "civilization of love." That term made its first official appearance in the writings of Pope Paul VI. For Paul VI, the building of a "civilization of love" is consistently, if somewhat vaguely, linked to the establishment of a stable and lasting peace within the international order. In his 1977 "Message for the Celebration of the 'World Day of Peace,'" for example, he states that the peace forged by the civilization of love "makes its own ideal of civilization." Yet he insists that this ideal "is no dream, no utopia, no illusion." It is "possible," and its establishment is mankind's "duty."

With Pope John Paul II, the term took on a more specific, yet still largely conceptual, meaning. John Paul's 1994 "Letter to Families" contains

---

20 Ibid., p. 186.

perhaps his fullest account of the meaning and demands of the civilization of love. John Paul traces the origins of the term back to the Greek and Latin Fathers' description of the "domestic church."[21] But while they used the term in this limited ecclesiastical sense, John Paul insists it "has a particular significance for the present time." In his view, that significance can be glimpsed in the etymology of the word "civilization." Initially used to describe the "civic or political dimensions" of human life, it has been extended to include the full scope of "human culture . . . which in the final analysis is nothing else than the 'humanization of the world.'" Viewed in this light, "civilization" is synonymous with "culture." It is thus possible to speak of a "culture of love." Originating "in the revelation of the God who 'is love,'" this "culture" would transcend the particularized, visible limits of the political community and the domestic church and incorporate and unite all of humanity. John Paul's stirring vision of a civilization of love provides a salutary and much-needed corrective to modernity's ruthless individualism.

However, the inherent depoliticizing tendencies of this view of the civilization of love are revealed most clearly in John Paul's 2004 "Message for the World Day of Peace." At the conclusion of that address, he notes true peace requires that "justice finds its fulfillment in charity."[22] But John Paul does not limit his treatment of the need for justice to be perfected by charity to the operations of charity on the individual man's soul or the community of men incorporated into the Body of Christ. Rather, he states (with an eye especially to the religious and political tensions in the Middle East) that "justice is not enough." For this reason, "the establishment of true peace in the world" requires charity. Indeed, charity must "enliven every sector of human life and extend to the international order." Only a world modeled on "the civilization of love," John Paul firmly concludes, "will be able to enjoy authentic and lasting peace."

Such statements call needed attention to the imperfections that plague and will forever continue to plague life within the earthly city. True justice, as Augustine never tired of pointing out, only reigns in the City of God. But the practical problem of imperfect justice in human affairs is not solved by transcending the realms of political justice and political life altogether. By directing the political and international order to an eschatological horizon where justice is perfected by charity, such statements put unrealistic weight and expectations on the limited but genuine good that can justly be achieved in political life. To say the least, it is difficult to see

[21] Pope John Paul II, "Letter to Families" (February 2, 1994), 13. All references to this address in this paragraph are to this section.

[22] Pope John Paul II, "Message for the World Day of Peace" (January 1, 2004), 10. All references to this address in this paragraph are to this section.

how the spiritual and transpolitical society of men bound together in charity and worship of God can be a model for either national or international politics. This is especially true given Christianity's traditional teaching on the disordering effects sin has on man and the political communities he founds. It may at times be possible to forge an uneasy temporal peace among nations, given the careful exercise of prudence by statesmen and the formation and recognition of reasonably just international laws. But what would it even mean, let alone look like, to have *love* among nations? Justice, as John Paul points out, is certainly not enough. On its own, the virtue of justice cannot perfect man as man, let alone substitute for the life of faith, hope, and charity that contributes to the ultimate perfection and happiness of human beings. And yet justice is the indispensable and proper virtue of political life, both in and among nations. The recognition of the true end of the civilization of love undoubtedly points to the intractable limits of life within the earthly city. But for this very reason, it cannot ever become a goal of the earthly city.

This point has been clearly restated by Pope Benedict XVI in his encyclical *Deus Caritas Est.*[23] Benedict states that the "entire activity of the Church is an expression of a love that seeks the integral good of man" (19). Grounded in the love of God, Christian charity imbues and informs the "service that the Church carries out in order to attend constantly to man's suffering and his needs, including material needs." Christ's injunction to love one's neighbor as himself is thus a responsibility for each individual Christian and for "the entire ecclesiastical community at every level." And yet because it moves *through* the particular men and women incorporated into the Mystical Body of Christ, the charitable "social service" the Church carries out in the world is a spiritual and a concrete reality. Echoing Augustine's treatment of the order of charity in *On Christian Doctrine*, the Pope refers to this movement as "a well-ordered love of neighbor" (§20). Such an order unites all those who belong to the Church with Christ and each other and ultimately aims to bring men into true, lasting communion with God in eternal life.

Benedict is careful to point out the relation between justice and charity. In doing so, he acknowledges "the Church's leadership was slow to realize that the issue of the just structuring of society needed to be approached in a new way" (§27). The rise of the modern state brought about "new situations and issues." The body of "Catholic social teaching," as he goes on to say, was "gradually developed" in order to respond to this new social, economic, and

---

23 Pope Benedict XVI, *God Is Love: Deus Caritas Est* (San Francisco: Ignatius Press, 2006).

political situation. The shift away *from* the political and *to* the social order in Catholic social thought did not mark any fundamental change in the Church's traditional understanding of the relation of political to social life. The Church continues to teach that, while each "human community possesses a common good which permits it to be recognized as such," it is nevertheless "in the *political community* that [the common good's] most complete realization is found."[24] This shift of emphasis reflected the Church's attempt to address a new kind of regime, modern democracy, which works in an unprecedented way to order life around the lines of a variegated civil society.

To appreciate the prudential character of this shift is to recognize the danger in believing that the appearance of the social encyclical *Rerum Novarum* marked the precise moment when the Catholic Church began to understand the political order—and its relation to it—in a wholly new way. The body of Catholic social teachings was not meant to provide a comprehensive and perfectly coherent Catholic "philosophy" or theology of democratic politics. It was not proffered as *the* solution to the theologico-political problem. Rather, it provided a way in which the Church could articulate its prudential rapprochement with liberal democracy.

Drawing attention to Christianity's "fundamental" recognition of the distinct, yet related, realms of Caesar and God, Benedict affirms that the "just ordering of society is . . . a central responsibility of politics" (§28). Since justice is "both the aim and the intrinsic criterion of politics," the political community cannot be reduced to a mere administrative mechanism that parcels out the material goods needed for human life. Nor can it be reduced to a juridical body of laws. The political community is responsible for preserving and cultivating the common good and for leading citizens to a life of virtue. It is also charged with arriving at some (admittedly imperfect) adjudication of the various claims to justice "arising from the different social forces" within it. As Manent has pointed out, for this reason the political *community* as *political* community is "the great mediation or the mediation of mediations."[25] As such, it allows the various social forces within the political community to communicate with one another and consequently prevents any one of these forces from absolutizing itself.

The Church does not sit idly by as a mere witness to this great mediation. It has much to say about the nature of justice, even the nature of justice in human affairs. On the basis of reason and natural law, the Church can (and must) articulate the basic, unchanging principles of justice that must be acknowledged by any legitimate political society. But by engaging in this pedagogical task, the Church is not arrogating to itself the

24 *Catechism of the Catholic Church*, 1910.

25 Manent, *A World Beyond Politics?*, p. 201.

"responsibility to make this teaching prevail in political life" (§28), says Benedict. "Rather, the Church wishes to help form consciences in political life and to stimulate greater insight into the authentic requirements of justice as well as greater readiness to act accordingly."

It must not be overlooked that Benedict presents these reflections on the nature of justice and political life in an encyclical titled *Deus Caritas Est.* In reflecting on the natures of eros and agape and their relation to each other, the Pope addresses the proper relation of faith, philosophy, morality, and politics. Reflecting on the significance that through faith Christians "have come to know and to believe in the love God has for us," the Pope is naturally led to raise questions that cut to the very heart of the theologico-political problem. The pursuit of these questions eventually leads to the conclusion that Christianity does provide a genuine solution to the humanly irresolvable theologico-political problem. While it affirms the indispensability and natural desirability of man's life within the earthly city, that solution remains fundamentally transpolitical. It is found in the City of God.

How then should we begin to think about the relationship between Catholicism and modern democracy? As I have tried to show, we must do so dialectically. Given modernity's inherent desire to resolve the theologico-political problem, Catholic political thought today must renew its appreciation of Augustine's teaching on the distinction between the earthly city and the City of God. Because it does not absolutize politics, Augustine's doctrine of the two cities avoids the monadic temptations of ideological totalitarianism and theocratic despotism. By drawing sharp lines between the temporal and the eternal, and the political and the spiritual, Augustine calls attention to the fact that politics is an inherently limited enterprise and that man ultimately longs for a form of wholeness that transcends the political order. As the brutal political history of the twentieth century attests, late modern man especially needs to be reminded of that important but often neglected lesson. Never losing sight of man's transpolitical destiny, Augustine's "political" thought exposes the naïveté of the humanly destructive belief—whether rooted in Christian apocalyptic or humanitarian convictions—that man and his institutions can ever eradicate evil on a societal level. By pointing to the limits of political life, his political thought calls attention to the earthly city's dependence on the City of God for its sustained, healthy existence. And it emphasizes the moral life's dependence on Christ and the virtue of charity for its ultimate theoretical and practical coherence.

Since late modern man is tempted to flee from the concrete particularities of the political order and seek refuge in some abstract realm of universal humanity, he needs to be reminded of the noble realities and requirements of political life. Catholic political thought therefore must also recover an appreciation of Aquinas's teachings on natural law and the desirability of political life. Over and against philosophic liberalism's insistence upon the constructed nature of morality and political life, Aquinas shows that morality is rooted in the natural order and that political life has its own legitimacy and natural desirability. His Christian Aristotelianism is able to explain why the good that is pursued in the political order is superior to the good that is pursued in either the family or society broadly and vaguely conceived. Aquinas's political thought additionally exposes the error of those Christians who, like the ancient Donatists, are only too eager to radicalize the Gospel and transform their religion into a rabidly antipolitical faith. By thinking through the moral and political implications of creation, he illuminates the natural foundations of morality and political life. In so doing, he shows why Christianity cannot view the political order as inherently corrupt and contributing nothing substantial to man's temporal felicity and his progress in virtue.

Catholic political thought must be able to think about the two poles of Christian citizenship—the Augustinian and Thomistic—*together* if it is to understand the religion's true relation to the political order. Despite their different and at times conflicting approaches, Augustine and Aquinas jointly reveal the full range of concerns that inform Christianity's response to the theologico-political question. Awareness of these concerns can help Catholic thinkers to understand why their religion can only forge a prudential accommodation with the modern liberal regime. As Augustine and Aquinas *both* show, Christianity does not oppose liberty or democracy per se, but the exaggerated and tendentially dehumanizing claims made about freedom and democracy by philosophic modernity. As a friendly critic of liberal democracy, Catholic political thought can affirm what is genuinely good about liberty and democracy and simultaneously refuse to affirm, in contrast to the modern state, that these are the highest or only human goods. By defending both the transpolitical nature of the Gospel and the natural desirability of political life, the two poles of Catholic political thought bring into sharper focus the humanizing limits and humanizing possibilities of life in the earthly city even as they point to the kingdom of God's fundamentally transpolitical solution to the problem of human living.

PART 2

John Courtney Murray and the American Proposition

CHAPTER 6

Life in the Late Republic: Catholic Role in America after Virtue

ARCHBISHOP CHARLES CHAPUT, O.F.M. CAP.
Archdiocese of Philadelphia

IN 1940, Fr. John Courtney Murray gave a series of three college talks. For his theme, he chose the "concept of a Christian culture." After his death, his Jesuit brothers fused the talks into a single essay called "The Construction of a Christian Culture."[1] It's a modest word change. But that title—the construction of a Christian culture—is a good place to begin our thoughts.

Most people know Murray for his work on Vatican II's *Decree on Religious Liberty*. In his 1960 book *We Hold These Truths*—which has never gone out of print—Murray argued the classic Catholic case for America. Like any important thinker, his work has friends and critics. The critics respect Murray's character and intellect. But they also tend to see him as a victim of his own optimism and a voice of American boosterism. I understand why. Over the years, too many people have used Murray to justify too many strange versions of personal conscience and the roles of church and state.

But for me, Murray's real genius is tucked inside his words from 1940. They are worth hearing again. Murray said that "a profound religious truth is at the basis of democratic theory and practice, namely the intrinsic dignity of human nature, the spiritual freedom of the human soul, its equality, as a soul, with others of its kind, and its superiority to all that does not share its spirituality." He said that "the task of constructing a culture is essentially spiritual, for culture has its home in the soul." As a

[1] John Courtney Murray, S.J., "The Construction of a Christian Culture," Woodstock Theological Center at Georgetown University, 1940, accessed December 12, 2011, woodstock.georgetown.edu/library/Murray/1940A.htm (all subsequent quotations of this document will be from this website).

result, "all man's cultural effort is at bottom an effort at submission to the truth and the beauty and the good that is outside him, existing in an ordered harmony, whose pattern he must produce within his soul by conformity with it."

These are beautiful thoughts. They are also true. The trouble is, they bear little likeness to our real culture today. Murray spoke at a moment when the word "gay" had more connection to joy than to sexual identity, and when the word "truth" could be used without ambivalence or irony. Times have changed.

We would all quickly get fatigued by a litany of what is gone strange with America. There is so much of it: from our consumerism and narcissism; to our sexual dysfunctions and family breakdowns; to our bad schools and moral illiteracy; to what Eric Voegelin called the "intellectual terrorism of institutions [like] the mass media, university departments, foundations and commercial publishing houses."[2] Listing problems and then complaining about them achieves little. And more importantly, as Murray would say, *it isn't a Christian response*. If Jesus tells us to be leaven in the world, and to make disciples of all nations—and, of course, he does—then we have missionary obligations. And those duties include the renewal of our country's best ideals.

But we cannot shape the future unless we know the facts of present-day life. And we cannot understand the present unless we know the past it came from. Reinhold Niebuhr once wrote that "memory is [the] fulcrum of freedom for man in history." The less we understand the past, "the more do present facts appear in the guise of irrevocable facts of nature."[3]

I believe that. And it explains some of the hardships American Catholics will now need to face. There is a passage in the Old Testament from the book of Judges. It says that after Joshua led the people across the Jordan and secured the Promised Land, "Joshua dismissed the people, [and] the sons of Israel went each to his heritage to take possession of the land. And the people served the LORD all the days of Joshua, and all the days of the elders who outlived Joshua, who had seen all the great work which the LORD had done for Israel." But after Joshua died, "all that generation also were gathered to their fathers; and there arose another generation after them, who did not know the LORD or the work which he had done for Israel" (2:6–7, 10).

---

[2] Eric Voegelin, "Why Philosophize? To Recapture Reality!" in *The Collected Works of Eric Voegelin, Volume 34: Autobiographical Reflections* (Columbia, Mo.: University of Missouri Press, 2006), p. 119.

[3] Reinhold Niebuhr, *Faith and History* (New York: Charles Scribner and Sons, 1949), p. 19.

The people of Israel forgot their God because they were not taught. And if American Catholics no longer know their faith, or its obligations of discipleship, or its call to mission—then we as leaders, parents, and teachers have no one to blame but ourselves.

Having said that, let me offer a portrait of our current terrain in very broad strokes.

I grew up in Kansas. And when I began my book *Render Unto Caesar* in 2006, I had in my mind the America I always knew—or thought I knew. But *that* America, I admit, has been passing for many years. When major Protestant and Catholic scholars—public intellectuals like Robert George and Timothy George, men with national weight—felt in 2009 that a manifesto like the Manhattan Declaration was needed, it affected me.

In its urgency for defending the sanctity of life and the dignity of marriage and the family, and the rights of religious conscience, the Manhattan Declaration came as a caution—for me, and for many other people—that a certain kind of America no longer exists.

This is ironic. Back in the 1930s, after visiting the United States, the great Lutheran pastor Dietrich Bonhoeffer wrote: "American democracy is founded not upon the emancipated man, but, quite the contrary, upon the kingdom of God and limitation of all earthly powers by the sovereignty of God."[4] The great British historian Paul Johnson said much the same—that America was "born Protestant"—and for good reason: America's earliest settlers were children of the Reformation. The Enlightenment ideas that helped shape America's foundation were themselves, in part, a product of earlier Christian thought. And Gov. John Winthrop's historic homily, "A Model of Christian Charity," given to Puritan colonists before leaving for the New World in 1630, expressed in a moving way the moral vision that has ever since flavored the American experiment. In a sense, America is not really the child of 1776 but of Reformation theologies and their results.

These Protestant roots have given us many good fruits: a culture of personal opportunity and freedom, respect for the individual, religious liberty, and reverence for the law. Other effects have been less happy: radical individualism, revivalist politics, a Calvinist hunger for material success as proof of salvation, and a nearly religious sense of national destiny and redemptive mission.

Our Enlightenment roots pose another problem. In America and Britain, the Enlightenment took a form tolerant and even friendly toward

---

[4] Dietrich Bonhoeffer, *Ethics* (New York: Macmillan, 1978), p. 104; text also appears in his collected writings, *No Rusty Swords* (Nashville, Tenn.: Abingdon Press, 1977).

religion. In France it turned harsh and antireligious. But as scholars Peter Gay and Jonathan Israel have separately argued, there was essentially only *one* Enlightenment in its basic principles. And it was fundamentally antireligious and specifically *anti-Christian*.[5] If this is true, then the main factor muting Enlightenment prejudice in America has been our tradition of widespread religious belief. And if faith declines, then hostility to religion must rise.

What is most striking about the American founding, of course, is the absence of any large Catholic role. The different strands in our nation's early history had one common theme: hostility to the Catholic Church. That prejudice, in one form or another, has continued down to the present day. As a result, Catholics, *as Catholic believers*, have always been strangers in a strange land.

The American Founders wanted to create a novus ordo seclorum, "a new order of the ages." But they had a strong sense of original sin. They also knew that history matters. Man cannot be reinvented out of nothing. Nor can he be made perfect by his own devices. So they borrowed heavily from a reliable source: Roman republican forms, law, institutions, architecture, and virtues. When friends called Charles Carroll—the only Catholic signer of the Declaration of Independence—an "American Cicero," it was the highest form of praise. (Bradley Birzer notes this, by the way, in his very good, new Carroll biography.)[6] Comparisons between Rome and America therefore make sense.

The differences, of course, are obvious. Rome was always a slave-dependent, agrarian society. It was never a "democracy" in the Athenian or modern American sense, much less an industrial power. But the similarities are also important, starting with structures of law and public life—but also with the fact that success bears the seeds of its own failure, and power corrupts.

As St. Augustine noted in *The City of God*, Roman success was built not just on greed, pride, and violence; it also flowed from the early Roman virtues of piety, austerity, courage, justice, and self-mastery. For Augustine, these virtues had an unfortunate and self-defeating basis in paganism. But in their natural effects, they were wholesome—so long as the Romans actually practiced them. All of these Roman virtues were revered in the thinking of the American Founders.

As with Rome, the fruits of American power now surround us. But success has always its cost in personal and national illusions. As a people,

---

[5] See Jonathan Israel, *Radical Enlightenment* (Oxford, Oxford University Press, 2001); *Enlightenment Contested* (Oxford: Oxford University Press, 2006); and Peter Gay, *The Enlightenment: The Rise of Modern Paganism*, rev. ed. (New York: W. W. Norton and Company, 1995).

[6] See Bradley J. Birzer, *American Cicero: The Life of Charles Carroll* (Wilmington, Del.: Intercollegiate Studies Institute, 2010).

we seem to become more foreign to our origins every year. The quality of education is declining. So is religious practice. Mediating institutions are diminishing. The size of government is growing. So is public and personal debt. Government and economic structures often seem remote and complex. The realities of American life—as the late Christopher Lasch argued—have created "a culture of narcissism" that seems to foster anxiety, self-absorption, and dependency.

Augustine's view of Rome can have an unpleasantly modern ring: he wrote that "[The pagans] are nowise concerned that the republic be less depraved and licentious. Only let it remain undefeated, they say, only let it flourish and abound in resources; let it be glorious by its victories, or still better, secure in peace; and what matters it to us? *This* is our concern: that every man be able to increase his wealth so as to supply his daily prodigalities."[7]

Of course, American politics has always been messy. This is not new. It is the nature of ordered liberty. But in the long run, a healthy civic life depends on permanent virtues rooted in nature's God, not "values" developed by ourselves. To their credit, nearly all of the Founders saw government as grounded in a divine authority greater than citizens themselves.

St. Augustine believed that political action and public service could be worthy Christian paths, *so long as* they are guided by the Christian virtues of faith, hope, and charity, and a humble awareness of human limits. So it would be bracing to imagine his thoughts about America in our current time—a nation where politics often seems dominated by market research, judicial activism, the ascendancy of positive law, lobbying, the vast expense of campaigning, simplified messaging, the complexity of government structures, party tribalism, and a dumbing down of the electorate.

American democracy needs an intelligent, reasoning citizenry—persons with free will and the maturity to use it. Yet American students now often fail to compete in global comparisons because of failures in public education. As Daniel Boorstin warned many years ago (1961), technological changes in our mass media—in the ways we deliver information—have had other, unintended consequences. Technology has modified the tools and the "language" of our public discourse, and therefore the way Americans think, feel, and act. To put it another way, America was created and sustained by a print culture. It is really not clear how well its institutions and traditions can survive in an electronic, image-oriented, technologically transformed world.[8]

---

7 St. Augustine, *The City of God*, Book 2, chap. 20.

8 See Daniel Boorstin, *The Image: A Guide to Pseudo-Events in America* (New York: Vintage, 1992); originally published in 1961.

These issues are compounded by declines in attention span and popular print literacy, the centralization of media ownership, rising costs and the need for profit, less time and resources available to journalists, and the drift away from professional skill and ideological detachment in newsrooms. As a result, many citizens experience reality from inside a media cocoon of entertainment and simplified news, while vital information and context go unreported.

Now, I have offered you a hard portrait. But I think we serve the truth by *telling* the truth as best we can. On Sundays we celebrate the Risen Christ, the real source of our freedom and joy. Christian faith in the Risen Jesus converted an empire. It changed the course of history and gave meaning to an entire civilization. And in the Risen Christ, I believe God is now calling us to do the same.

The integration of faith and reason in Western culture has ensured its humanity and genius. America's welcome of religious faith among its people has been the key to its decency and vitality. But we need to remember Leszek Kolakowski's warning that the words of the Declaration of Independence "We hold these truths to be self-evident" are *not at all* self-evident to the modern intellectual world.[9] We also need to remember J. L. Talmon's caution that democracy too can become "totalitarian."[10]

The inquisitors of today's developed societies are secular, not religious. The real enemies of human freedom, greatness, imagination, art, hope, culture, and conscience are those who attack religious belief, not believers. Real hope—not empty optimism but the *virtue* of hope, the virtue Georges Bernanos called "despair, overcome"—is impossible without faith in realities unseen. Unbelief—whether deliberate and ideological, or lazy and pragmatic—is the state religion of the modern world. The fruit of that orthodoxy is a compression and destruction of the human spirit, and a society without higher purpose. This is the logic of the choices that America is already making. But they can be unmade. And they can be redeemed.

I want to close by going back to John Courtney Murray. As I said earlier, Murray is sometimes seen as being too high on America, too naïve about its flaws, and too grand about its possibilities. And he truly did love the best ideals of our country, because those ideals are worthy of honor. But in "The Construction of a Christian Culture," he also said this:

---

9 Leszek Kolakowski, *Modernity on Endless Trial* (Chicago: University of Chicago Press, 1990), p. 146.

10 See J. L. Talmon, *The Origins of Totalitarian Democracy* (New York: W. W. Norton and Company, 1970).

> American culture, as it exists, is actually the quintessence of all that is decadent in the culture of the Western Christian world. It would seem to be erected on the triple denial that has corrupted Christian culture at its roots, the denial of metaphysical reality, the primacy of the spiritual over the material, of the social over the individual. . . . Its most striking characteristic is its profound materialism. . . . It has given citizens everything to live for and nothing to die for. And its achievement may be summed up thus: It has gained a continent and lost its own soul.

In the same text he says, "[I]n view of the fact that American culture is built on the negation of all that Christianity stands for, it would seem that our first step toward the construction of a Christian culture should be the destruction of the existing one. In the presence of a Frankenstein, one does not reach for baptismal water, but for a bludgeon."

He wrote those words decades ago. We can only guess what he might write today.

For Murray, there is no *real* "humanism" without the cross of Jesus Christ. And dismantling the inhuman parody we call "modern American culture" begins not with violence but with the conversion of our own hearts. This is the only kind of revolution that lasts, the only kind with the power to change everything. The problem in American Catholic life is not a lack of money or resources or personnel or social influence. These things can be important, but they are never fundamental.

The central problem in constructing a Christian culture is our lack of faith and the cowardice it produces. We need to admit this. And then we need to submit ourselves to a path of repentance and change, and unselfishly witness to others. The reality of life in the late years of the American republic is that "we have sought first the kingdom of earth," as Murray said, "and we begin to discover that in the process, millions upon millions have been disinherited from both the kingdom of earth and the Kingdom of God."

The role of Catholics in America is *exactly the opposite* of what we have been doing for half a century or more—compromising too cheaply, assimilating, fitting in, fleeing from who we really are as believers, and in the process being bleached out and digested by the culture we were sent to make holy.

C. S. Lewis once famously said that Christianity is a "fighting religion."[11] He did not mean a religion of violence. He meant that Christianity is a religion of candor in naming good and evil, zeal in advancing the

---

[11] C. S. Lewis, *Mere Christianity* (New York: HarperCollins ed., 2001), first published in 1952.

Gospel of Jesus Christ, and courage in struggling against sin. Our task as Catholics in the years ahead is to strengthen that spirit in each other—and to instill it in all the people we reach with the extraordinary skills God has given us. If we do *only that,* but do it well, then God will do the rest.

Murray said, "Only when our dwelling is in the heavens can we hope to fulfill our vocation on earth. . . . If we do not understand the world and why it was made, what right have we to meddle with it? If we do not know that man is made in the image of God, how dare we . . . attempt to fashion his life?"

The construction of a Christian culture begins by lifting our own hearts up to God, without plans or reservations, and letting him begin the work. It sounds like a small thing; it is a small thing. But as Christians know better than anyone, worlds and empires can turn on the smallest yes.

CHAPTER 7

Truths Still Held? John Courtney Murray's "American Proposition" Fifty Years Later

GEORGE WEIGEL
Ethics and Public Policy Center, Washington, D.C.

ALTHOUGH WRITTEN decades ago, Fr. John Courtney Murray's *We Hold These Truths: Catholic Reflections on the American Proposition* is arguably the most important such reflection composed in our time, and perhaps in any time. Its publication landed Father Murray, an urbane New York Jesuit, on the cover of *Time*, in the days when that distinction, like the Nobel Peace Prize, actually meant something. Reviewing the book in the January 28, 1961, issue of *National Review*, William F. Buckley Jr. described Murray and his work in these glowing terms: "A man with commanding knowledge and piercing intuition who . . . speaks to his . . . fellow Americans from breathtaking heights whence he surveys the American and the world scene, creating thought and analysis which leave the reader stunned with admiration and pleasure, as only the contact with a great thinker and a fine writer can do." A few years later, Murray's reputation was such that Cardinal Francis Spellman of New York brought him to the Second Vatican Council as a peritus, or official theological adviser, so that Murray's historical and political-philosophical work on Church-state theory could help shape the Council's deliberations on religious freedom—which it did, if not quite as decisively as some have suggested (or in precisely the way Murray would have wished).

We Hold These Truths was not without its critics, then or now. Some argued that Murray's account of the American Founding massively reduced the role of biblical religion, and especially Calvinist thought, on the national consensus that produced the new republic. Others, more now than then, suggested that Murray's theory of democracy was based on an excessively Neo-Scholastic (meaning, specifically, Suarezian) reading of the relationship between nature and grace—a charge denied by Fr. Francis Canavan, S.J., who argued that Murray was writing about politics, not theology. Some scholars accept Canavan's distinction but argue that Murray's theory of democracy was too much beholden to John Locke. Still others find in Murray's address to specific questions of public policy in the mid-1960s the opening wedge to what might be called Cuomoism among Catholic public officials—a charge that, in the final analysis, does a disservice to Murray even as it gives an undeserved intellectual gloss to Mario Cuomo and those theologians and lawyers who helped turn the Kennedy clan into advocates for so-called reproductive choice.

For a man who was America's most prominent Catholic public intellectual in 1965, when Vatican II adopted the Declaration on Religious Freedom his work had helped make possible, Murray went into strikingly rapid eclipse after his untimely death in 1967 from a longstanding heart ailment. A younger Jesuit generation, drinking deeply from the Kool-Aid of the Sixties (rather than from Murray's favorite "Beefeater martini, desperately dry"), jettisoned Murray as impossibly old hat, claiming, as one put it, that "we know so much more than Murray did." After twenty years of neglect however, Murray was resurrected in the mid-1980s by Catholic thinkers seeking materials from which to build a religiously informed public philosophy for the American experiment in ordered liberty. This, in turn, led to an effort, perhaps not surprising, to reclaim Murray for "progressive" Catholicism—a project risible to anyone familiar with the (often hilarious) stories of Murray's contempt for some of the woollier-headed notions being circulated at Woodstock College in the years before his death (and Woodstock's demise).

My purpose here, however, is not to sort out the arguments over Murray's analysis of the Founding, and still less his metaphysics and epistemology, but to review the "American Proposition" he sketched in *We Hold These Truths* as a template for measuring the health of the American republic and its public culture as we enter the second decade of the twenty-first century. That template has its own validity and utility, irrespective of where one stands on the questions of Murray-as-historian-of-the-Founding or Murray-the-Neo-Scholastic.

The Proposition

The opening paragraphs of Murray's book summarize its argument and give the flavor of his cool, dry rhetorical style:

> It is classic American doctrine, immortally asserted by Abraham Lincoln, that the new nation which our Fathers brought forth on this continent was dedicated to a "proposition".
>
> I take it that Lincoln used the word with conceptual propriety. In philosophy a proposition is the statement of a truth to be demonstrated. In mathematics, a proposition is at times the statement of an operation to be performed. Our Fathers dedicated the nation to a proposition in both of these senses. The American Proposition is at once doctrinal and practical, a theorem and a problem. It is an affirmation and also an intention. It presents itself as a coherent structure of thought that lays claim to intellectual assent; it also presents itself as an organized political project that aims at historical success. Our Fathers asserted it and most ably argued it; they also took to "work it out," and they signally succeeded.
>
> Neither as a doctrine nor as a project is the American Proposition a finished thing. Its demonstration is never done once for all; and the Proposition itself requires development on penalty of decadence. Its historical success is never to be taken for granted, nor can it come to some absolute term; and any given measure of success demands enlargement on penalty of instant decline. In a moment of national crisis Lincoln asserted the imperiled part of the theorem and gave impetus to the impeded part of the project in the noble utterance, at once declaratory and imperative, "All men are created equal." Today, when civil war has become the basic fact of world society, there is no element of the theorem that is not menaced by active negation, and no thrust of the project that does not meet powerful opposition. Today therefore thoughtful men among us are saying that America must be more clearly conscious of what it proposes, more articulate in proposing, more purposeful in the realization of the project proposed.[1]

This "American Proposition," as Murray understood it, was a "conservation"-by-development of the political dimension of the Western civilizational project that had emerged over the centuries from the fruitful interaction of Jerusalem, Athens, and Rome: that is, of biblical religion, Greek rationality, and Roman law. As such, the Proposition rested on a realist epistemology: there are truths built into the world and into us; we can know those truths through the arts of reason; knowing those truths, certain obligations, both personal and civil, are laid upon us. To be sure, those truths had to be "held, assented to, worked into the texture of institutions," in order for there to be a "true City, in which men may dwell in

[1] John Courtney Murray, S.J., *We Hold These Truths: Catholic Reflections on the American Proposition* (Garden City, N.Y.: Doubleday Image Books, 1964), p. 1.

dignity, peace, unity, justice, well-being, [and] freedom."[2] But that never-to-be-taken-for-granted quality of the truths of the American Proposition simply underscored the fact that the United States was an experiment: an experiment in ordered freedom.

That could be said, I suppose, of any democracy; and the perils attending any democracy's failure to order its public life by the moral truths we can know to be true were chillingly demonstrated by Weimar Germany and, to a lesser degree of horror, by the French Third Republic. What was, and is, distinctive about American democracy, however, is that our very nationhood depends on our purchase of the truths to which the Founders pledged their lives, fortunes, and sacred honor. The German nation remained after the collapse of the Weimar Republic; France remained France under the Vichy regime. America was different, Murray argued. For America's native condition was plurality and the American people—the American nation—had to be constructed, not out of the old materials of blood and ethnicity and language and soil and common religious conviction, but out of the new materials of adherence to truths in the civic order. The survival of America, as both theorem and project, rested on the American ability to create pluralism out of plurality: to transform the native cacophony of ethnic and religious difference into an orderly conversation about public goods, the "order" being provided by common allegiance to the elementary truths of the Proposition.

Murray's theory of democracy, while seeming thin to some of his critics, was thus far thicker than that of today's democratic functionalists, whose sole concern is to get the machinery of governance right. Murray, by contrast, thought of politics, not as machinery, but as deliberation—common deliberation, among men and women who were citizens and not merely bundles of desires; common deliberation about public goods, using the arts of reason in order to apply agreed-upon first principles of truth in the civic order to the exigencies of governance amidst the flux of history. In this conception of democracy, civility and tolerance were moral accomplishments, not poses, attitudes, or pragmatic accommodations. Tolerance meant not differences ignored but differences engaged. Civility was the achievement of a measure of order (and thus a measure of clarity, and perhaps even charity) in the public conversation.

Nor, contrary to others of his critics, was Murray's democratic theory overly dependent on a Hobbesian or Lockean construal of civil society:

> We no longer believe, with Locke or Hobbes, that man escapes from a mythical "state of nature" by an act of will, by a social contract.

[2] Ibid., p. 9.

> Civil society is a need of human nature before it becomes the object of human choice. Moreover, every particular society is a creation of the soil; it springs from the physical soil of earth and from the more formative soil of history. Its existence is sustained by loyalties that are not logical; its ideals are expressed in legends that go beyond the facts and are for that reason vehicles of truth . . . nevertheless, the distinctive bond of [civil society] is reason, or, more exactly, that exercise of reason which is argument.[3]

Argument, in turn, gave form to a distinctive kind of association in the American democratic experiment. Jacques Maritain might have called it "civic friendship." A generation after Murray, John Paul II would call it "solidarity." It was, Murray wrote, a "special kind of moral virtue, a thing of reason and intelligence, laboriously cultivated by the [disciplining] of passion, prejudice, and narrow self-interest."[4] This was not the friendship of David and Jonathan, or the fierce inclusiveness of the clan or tribe; it was not the bond of charity that binds disciples within the Church. It was a solidarity, a civic friendship, born of a common passion for justice, with the requirements of justice—what is owed by the City to the citizenry, and what citizens owe the City—understood according to the canons of public reason. And in the pursuit of justice would be found the perfecting of civility.

The bonds of this civic friendship or solidarity in America reinforced that founding consensus that gave philosophical content to Murray's American Proposition. This consensus was, in Murray's words, "an ensemble of substantive truths, a structure of basic knowledge, an order of elementary affirmations" that reflect the truths we can and must know by reason about how we ought to live together.[5] No true City, and certainly no true democracy, is possible if everything is in doubt. If there is to be genuine argument, and not just cacophony or the will-to-power, there must be, Murray wrote, "a core of agreement, accord, concurrence, acquiescence," because only if certain truths are held can there be genuine arguments.[6] Much of modernity, Murray knew, had this exactly backwards, thinking that argument ends when agreement is reached. The opposite is more fundamentally true, in both the sciences and the humanities: real argument is only possible within a preexisting context of agreement on certain truths.

This may sound daunting, but we need not discover these truths by our own labors alone. Rather, the truths that form the moral-cultural

---

3 Ibid., p. 19.

4 Ibid.

5 Ibid., p. 21.

6 Ibid.

foundations of American democracy come to us as a patrimony—an inheritance to be honored and cultivated—from the civilizational project of the West as it emerged over millennia: that inheritance that Pope Leo XIII, founder of modern Catholic social doctrine, called the *patrimonium generis humani*. It was not a finished thing, this patrimony; it had, Murray argued, a "growing end."[7] But the development that we, the inheritors, were to cultivate through civil argument had to be rooted in the inheritance of truth that gave distinction (in both senses of the term) to the Western civilizational project.

The Truths of the Proposition

What were the inherited truths on which the American experiment rested and by which the American civil argument was structured?

A nation under judgment. The first truth of the consensus that gave content to the American Proposition was a truth that "lies beyond politics . . . [and] imparts to politics a fundamental human meaning": the truth that God is sovereign over nations as well as over individuals. Here, like Edmund Burke, Murray distinguished the Anglo-American political tradition from the Jacobinism of continental European political philosophy. The latter began its thinking about politics with autonomous human reason; the former looked "to the sovereignty of God as to the first principle of its organization."[8] The American experiment, in other words, was an experiment under transcendent judgment: the judgment of the God of the Bible; the judgment of those moral truths inscribed by nature's God in nature—that is, in the world and in us—as a reflection of the divine creative purpose.

That "natural law," which we can know by reason, gave government the authority to command, even as it limited the powers of the governors. The constitutional agreement by which the people, through their representatives, ratified the basic instruments of American governance and amended that agreement as circumstances required was a process, as Murray understood it, by which "the people define the areas where [public] authority is legitimate and the areas where liberty is lawful."[9] Thus the U.S. Constitution and the various state constitutions both enumerated rights and laid out plans by which those rights might be lived in solidarity.

Consent. The second foundational truth of the American Proposition also grew out of the Christian civilization of the Middle Ages, rather than from the autonomy project of the Continental Enlightenment: the princi-

[7] Ibid., p. 22.
[8] Ibid., p. 40.
[9] Ibid., p. 44.

ple that all just governance is by and with the consent of the governed. On this reading of Western history, rather different from the Whig rendering, royal absolutism and its parallel union of altar-and-throne were the aberration; the rich social pluralism of the Middle Ages and the assumed limits on princely authority both reflected, in Murray's view, "the premise . . . that there is a sense of justice inherent in the people."[10]

This principle of consent, and its premise that the people can know the moral truths by which we ought to live together, again stands in sharp contrast to the Jacobin tradition in continental Europe and its twentieth-century manifestation, totalitarianism, which proposed governance by elite vanguards. The principle also assumes that there are truths to be known and truths that we can know in common to be true, rather than postmodernism's "your truth" and "my truth." But that is to get ahead of ourselves a bit.

The principle of consent and the premise of the people's sense of justice framed Murray's understanding of human rights, which posed another challenge to an autonomy-based theory of democracy:

> In the American concept of them . . . [the] institutions of [free speech and a free press] do not rest on the thin theory proper to eighteenth-century individualistic rationalism, that a man has a right to say what he thinks merely because he thinks it. The American agreement was to reject political censorship of opinion as unrightful, because unwise, imprudent, not to say impossible. However, the proper premise of these freedoms lay in the fact that they were social necessities. . . . They were regarded as conditions essential to the conduct of free, representative, and responsible government. People who are called upon to obey have the right first to be heard. People who are to bear burdens and make sacrifices have the right first to pronounce on the purposes which their sacrifices serve. People who are summoned to contribute to the common good have the right first to pass judgment on the question, whether the good proposed be truly good, the people's good, the common good.[11]

In the American Proposition, in other words, rights were not trumps recognized as such by the sheer fact of their assertion. Rights were rooted in the dignity of the human person as capable of rational moral choice and considered political judgment. Rights were acknowledged in law to facilitate the promotion and defense of the common good, not simply to protect individual "choice."

---

[10] Ibid., p. 45.

[11] Ibid., pp. 45–46.

The priority of society. The third truth of the American Proposition also challenged both absolutism and the Jacobinism that sought to replace it, setting in motion the path toward totalitarianism: and that was the truth that, as Murray put it, "the state is distinct from society and limited in its offices toward society."[12] Or, to put it in slightly different language, society exists prior to the state, ontologically as well as historically, and the state exists to serve society, not the other way around.

Here, too, was another ground for such basic civil rights as free speech and a free press: "the principle of the incompetence of government in the field of opinion."[13] This retrieval of the medieval distinction between studium and imperium, the order of culture and the political order, would have large consequences for Murray's Church-state theory and indeed for the Second Vatican Council, which agreed with Murray's contention that the state was incompetent in theological matters, such that religious freedom was a right grounded in both the dignity of the person and the natural limits of the rightly ordered state. For our purposes, however, the salient point, as Murray put it, was that government, rightly understood, "submits itself to judgment by the truth of society; it is not itself a judge of the truth in society."[14] Nor, mutatis mutandis, is government the judge of the truths inscribed in nature, which give rise to what Murray called "the truth of society." Rightly ordered government submits itself to the judgment of those truths built into the world and into us, and if it attempts to redefine those truths, it has acted unjustly and illegitimately. The Polish bishops' heroic 1953 "*Non possumus*!" ["We cannot!"], spoken in defiance of an attempt by Poland's communist regime to make the Catholic Church a subsidiary of the party-state, was one modern example of resistance to this attempted arrogation of illegitimate power by the state; other such attempts are close at hand and will be discussed presently.

Freedom and virtue. The fourth component of the American Proposition was "the profound conviction that only a virtuous people can be free."[15] There were no guarantees about the success of freedom, Murray knew; freedom could dissipate into license, private license could lead to public decadence, and decadence could lead to the chaos out of which a new authoritarianism would emerge. "It is not an American belief," Murray wrote, that "the free government is inevitable, only that it is possible." Moreover, "its possibility can be realized only when the people as a whole are inwardly governed by the recognized imperatives of the universal

[12] Ibid., p. 46.
[13] Ibid.
[14] Ibid.
[15] Ibid., p. 47.

moral law."[16] Freedom and moral truth, Murray wrote in anticipation of the teaching of John Paul II in *Centesimus Annus*, are inextricably bound together: freedom must be tethered to truth and ordered to goodness if freedom is not to become its own undoing.

Murray applauded the ways in which the American cultural instinct for freedom (which had been forged from multiple sources—biblical, medieval, Puritan, and so forth) had succeeded over time in placing limits on the sphere of government within a functioning democracy. Both in personal moral decision making, however, and in sustaining civil society, the American demand for freedom could "be made with the full resonance of moral authority only to the extent that it issues from an inner sense of responsibility to a higher law."[17] Thus the American idea and the American ideal was *ordered* freedom: freedom ordered to goodness because it is tethered to truth. "Men who would be free politically must discipline themselves," Murray wrote; "political freedom is endangered in its foundations as soon as the universal moral values, upon whose shared possession the self-discipline of a free society depends, are no longer vigorous enough to restrain the passions and shatter the selfish inertia of men."[18] Democracy, in other words, could not be reduced to a matter of political mechanics; democracy was "a spiritual and moral enterprise."[19]

Truths Held, Then?

So, the sovereignty of God and of transcendent moral truth over nations as well as individuals, acknowledged through the people's possession of the truths of the natural moral law that bear on governance; the principle of consent, with its cousin, the principle of participation, grounded in the conviction that the people have with them an inherent sense of justice and giving rise to a thick notion of rights linked to both human dignity and civic responsibility; the priority of society over the state; the linkage between freedom and virtue and the ideal of *ordered* freedom—these were the consensus ideas that, in John Courtney Murray's view, informed and shaped the American Proposition as both a proposal and a project in history. How did Murray imagine them being held in his day, more than a half century ago?

He did not think the Proposition could be carried any longer by the primary institutions of its transmission between the colonial period and

[16] Ibid.
[17] Ibid.
[18] Ibid., p. 48.
[19] Ibid.

the Second World War: the Christian communities of the old Protestant mainline. The theological chaos in those quarters was such that no coherent account of the Proposition was likely to issue from, much less be transmitted by, the communities arrayed in what was then a formidable institution, the National Council of Churches.

Nor would the falling torch be picked up by the American academy, which had "long ago bade a quiet goodbye to the whole notion of an American consensus, as implying that there are truths that we hold in common, and a natural law that makes known to all of us the structure of the moral universe in such wise that all of us are bound by it to a common obedience."[20] Pragmatism and utilitarianism, then dominant on prestigious American campuses, could not give a compelling account of the Proposition. (Murray could not, of course, have anticipated the contemporary dominance of the academy by postmodernism's epistemological skepticism, metaphysical nihilism, and moral relativism; but it is not difficult to imagine the odds he would have given on that intellectual dog's breakfast being able to give a persuasive account of the American Proposition—or indeed any other proposition.)

Murray's suggestion—a striking one at a historical moment when considerable swaths of the American Protestant leadership believed that the United States had been and must be a Protestant country, and did so with a passion at least as fervent as Francisco Franco's convictions about the essential Catholicism of Spain—was that the originating and constituting consensus that had made America itself was still possessed by, and might be revived by, the Catholic community in the United States.

That revitalization was not to happen, as the Catholic Church lurched into the fever swamps of the Sixties and Seventies of the last century in what seems in retrospect to have been an attempt to catch up with the Protestant mainline, just as it was becoming the Protestant oldline en route to becoming the liberal Protestant sideline. The brakes were put on, eventually, not so much by ecclesiastical disciplinary measures but by the lucid and luminous social doctrine of John Paul II and its promulgation in the United States by various of the late Pope's disciples. But the opportunity Murray saw in the late Fifties and early Sixties was another victim of the immediate post-Vatican II silly season—although if we listen carefully, we can hear echoes today, and sometimes more than echoes, of the consensus ideas of the American Proposition in the pro-life advocacy of the Catholic Church in the United States and its new allies among the more thoughtful leadership of Evangelical Protestantism. (This recent alliance

[20] Ibid., p. 51.

would likely have come as something of a shock to Father Murray, but from his present station in the communion of saints he would, I think, appreciate both the ironies involved and the new possibilities of civil argument opened up by the rise of a new ecumenism.)

The Culture War

When, on the first page of *We Hold These Truths*, Father Murray referred to "civil war . . . [as] the basic fact of world society," he was thinking of the contest between imperfect democracies and the pluperfect tyranny of communism. The latter was sent onto the trash heap of history decades ago, by brave men and women, often inspired by Christian faith, who had come, by their own hard and distinctive paths, to an understanding of the "elementary affirmations" within the American Proposition as both truths to be affirmed and truths to be instantiated in history—thus demonstrating, I should note, the fact of a natural moral law that is universal in character. Yet the civil war continues; it is now prosecuted through what we call the American "culture war" and its analogues throughout the West. Murray, who did not use that term "culture war," clearly anticipated its possibility when he penned the following warning:

> Perhaps one day the noble many-storeyed mansion of democracy will be dismantled, leveled to the dimensions of a flat majoritarianism, which is no mansion but a barn, perhaps even a tool shed in which the weapons of tyranny may be forged. Perhaps there will one day be wide dissent even from the political principles which merge from natural law, as well as dissent from the constellation of ideas that have historically undergirded those principles—the idea that government has a moral basis; that the universal moral law is the foundation of society; that the legal order of society—that is, the state—is subject to judgment by a law that is not statistical but inherent in the nature of man; that the eternal reason of God is the ultimate origin of all law; that this nation in all its aspects—as a society, a state, an ordered and free relationships between governors and governed—is under God. The possibility that widespread dissent from these principles should develop is not foreclosed.[21]

Indeed not, for that possibility is now manifestly with us. But the foreclosure need not be complete, and the mansion need not be leveled or abandoned. Saving it, however, means facing squarely the various ways in which the truths of Murray's Proposition are no longer held.

[21] Ibid., p. 53.

Truths Held Now?

It might seem that the first truth of the Proposition—the sovereignty of God over nations as well as individuals, with its parallel conviction about the universal moral law inscribed in nature and accessible to reason—would be most gravely threatened by the so-called new atheism. But as David Bentley Hart bracingly demonstrates in *Atheist Delusions: The Christian Revolution and Its Fashionable Enemies*, the attacks of Richard Dawkins, Christopher Hitchens, Sam Harris, and Daniel Dennett, and their down-market cash-out in Dan Brown's *Da Vinci Code*, do not get us to the true root of the problem, which is not the historically ill-informed and philosophically embarrassing "new atheism," but rather what Romano Guardini used to call the "interior disloyalty of modern times," which is a betrayal of "the structure of reality itself."[22]

This betrayal is most powerfully embodied, not by such relative lightweights as Dawkins, Hitchens, Dennett, Harris, et alia, but by postmodernism's skepticism about the human capacity to know the truth of anything with certainty, a skepticism that, as mentioned above, yields, on the one hand, metaphysical nihilism, and, on the other, moral relativism. Indeed, according to a trenchant reading of modernity by the French philosopher Rémi Brague, nihlism may be the defining challenge of this cultural moment in the West. For in Brague's analysis, the twenty-first century will be the century of being-and-nothingness, as the twentieth century (defined by the contest with totalitarianism) was the century of true-and-false and the nineteenth (defined by the "social question" emerging from the Industrial Revolution) was the century of good-and-evil. The metaphysical question—the question of loyalty to being itself—is the bottom of the cultural bottom line today, and in a way not seen since metaphysics emerged from the labors of Greek philosophy in the classical period.

In 1955, Flannery O'Connor wrote that "if you live today you breathe in nihilism."[23] Those who once found that complaint a bit extravagant might ponder the reality of contemporary nihilism through one of its recent public manifestations—the claim that the natural moral law we can know by reason is, in truth, a form of irrational bigotry and extremism. That claim was adduced on October 30, 2009, in the lead editorial of the *Washington Post*, written to cripple a candidate for attorney general of

---

22 Cited in ibid., p. 208. See also David Bentley Hart, *Atheist Delusions: The Christian Revolution and Its Fashionable Enemies* (New Haven, Conn.: Yale University Press, 2009).

23 Sally Fitzgerald, ed., *The Habit of Being: Letters of Flannery O'Connor* (New York: Farrar Straus Giroux, 1979), p. 97.

Virginia, Ken Cuccinelli, whose defense of natural law as an instrument for formulating public policy was decried by the sometimes-sensible editors of the nation's leading political newspaper as a "retrofit (of) the old language of racism, bias, and intolerance in a new context."[24] That the "new context" in question was the gay insurgency and its demands that the state recognize gay unions as "marriages" was, in a sense, beside the point (although it illustrated the degree to which the abandonment of any natural law approach to the question of what constitutes a marriage soon leads to intellectual meltdown); the same charge of irrational bigotry could have been adduced had the issue been the first principle of justice that tells us that abortion and euthanasia are morally wrong.

But, for my purposes here, as we assay the health of our political culture through the template of Murray's American Proposition, what was truly stunning about the *Post*'s editorial assault on natural law was its implicit willingness to throw out Jefferson's claims in the Declaration of Independence, Lincoln's claims in the Gettysburg Address, and Martin Luther King Jr.'s claims in his "Letter from Birmingham Jail," all of which appealed to a natural moral law that was a reflection of the eternal and divine law. To deny that such a moral law exists, and to compound that intellectual error by the moral crime of labeling those who still adhere to the first truth of the American Proposition as bigots, brought to mind Murray's cautions about the barbarism that threatened us:

> Barbarism is not . . . the forest primeval with all its relatively simple savageries. Barbarism . . . is the lack of reasonable conversation according to reasonable laws. Here the word "conversation" has its twofold Latin sense. It means living together and talking together.
>
> Barbarism threatens when men cease to live together according to reason, embodied in law and custom, and incorporated in a web of institutions. . . . Society becomes barbarian . . . when the ways of men come under the sway of the instinctual, the impulsive, the compulsive. When things like this happen, barbarism is abroad, whatever the surface impressions of urbanity.
>
> Barbarism likewise threatens when men cease to talk together according to reasonable laws. . . . Argument ceases to be civil . . . when defiance is flung to the basic ontological principle of all ordered discourse, which asserts that Reality is an analogical structure, within which there are variant modes of reality, to each of which corresponds a distinctive method of thought that imposes on argument its special rules. When things like this happen, men cannot be locked together in

[24] "Mr. Cuccinelli's Bigotry," *Washington Post*, October 30, 2009.

argument. Conversation becomes merely quarrelsome or querulous. Civility dies with the death of the dialogue.[25]

Barbarism masquerading as a defense of tolerance: that was what greeted readers of the *Washington Post* editorial page on the morning of October 30, 2009. That greeting was one ominous measure of the condition of the first truth in Murray's American Proposition.

As for the second truth—the principle of consent, which reflects the conviction that the people have an inherent sense of justice, and which is allied to the principle of participation that provides an account of the nature of our civil and political rights—one might think it in rather better shape. Elections in America take place regularly, however vulgarly. Public officials are rotated in and out of office, if not as often as some would like. Initiatives and referenda repair the damage that the people's inherent sense of justice tells them has been done to the common good by legislatures or courts. Free speech and freedom of the press are robust, if too often shallow. But the barbarians are among us on this front, too.

The most obvious instance of an assault on the principle of consent is what a *First Things* symposium termed, in 1996, the "judicial usurpation of politics." This violation of a constituting truth of the American Proposition was most egregious in *Roe v. Wade*; the degree to which the Supreme Court got it colossally wrong in *Roe* can be measured by the degree to which the effects of Roe have roiled our public life ever since (just as, in the past, the Court's colossal mistakes in *Dred Scott* and *Plessy v. Ferguson* distorted our public life for decades). By the same token, of course, the people's refusal to acquiesce to what their inherent sense of justice tells them is the fundamental injustice embodied in *Roe*'s virtually unfettered abortion license—a refusal that launched and sustains the pro-life movement—expresses the vitality of the second truth of the Proposition. Yet it is not easy to see how the mistake the Court made in *Roe* can be finally remedied until our public culture gains a firmer grip on the first truth of the Proposition. Until that day, there is important work to be done in mitigating the effects of *Roe*, as there will doubtless be efforts to reverse a grave error in constitutional judging. Both are welcome. Neither, however, will suffice to create an America in which every child is welcomed in life and protected in law; that requires a reclaiming of the truth that innocent life, at whatever stage and in whatever condition, has an intrinsic dignity and value that the law must acknowledge and protect. Meanwhile, the work of resistance to judicial usurpation—which effects our public life on

[25] Murray, *We Hold These Truths*, pp. 25–26.

virtually every front—will and must continue, in defense of the second truth of the Proposition.

It should also be noted, however, that there is a new assault on the second truth that bears careful watching, and to which resistance must be mounted: the censorship of rationally defensible moral judgment in the name of laws banning what some deem "hate speech." Such censorship, enforced by coercive state power, is already underway in Canada, where Christian ministers have been assessed significant fines for preaching classic biblical morality in the matter of homosexual acts, and in Europe, where the most widely circulated quality Catholic magazine in Poland was recently convicted by both a European human rights court and a Polish court of violating a woman's "rights" by reporting, accurately, that she had sought an abortion on grounds of not wanting to bear a severely near-sighted child. In the latter case, calling eugenics by its proper name seemed to two courts an expression of hate speech. We need not doubt that similar attempts to censor the truths of the Proposition will cross the 49th parallel heading south, and the Atlantic Ocean heading west. The degree of resistance that can be mounted to these efforts will be an important measure of the degree to which the truth of the principle of consent is still held in these United States.

That the third truth within the Proposition—that the state exists to serve society, which is ontologically and historically antecedent to the state—has become attenuated in its grip on our public culture seems clear from two recent controversies.

The first involved President Obama's commencement address on May 17, 2009, at the University of Notre Dame, when he made controversial comments regarding abortion.[26] It is beyond the scope of this book to explore the question of whether Notre Dame violated its own commitments as a Catholic institution of higher learning by holding up this president as an exemplar and by granting him an honorary doctorate of laws; my focus here is on what the president said, which was most remarkable, and most disturbing.

Controversies over the doctrinal and moral boundaries of communities of faith have been a staple of American life for centuries. The state of Rhode Island is the by-product of one of those controversies. Trinitarians battled Unitarianism within Congregationalism; Missouri Synod Lutherans and Wisconsin Synod Lutherans battled other kinds of Lutherans; Reform Judaism sought to distinguish itself dramatically from Orthodox Judaism,

[26] "Obama's Commencement Address at Notre Dame," *New York Times*, transcript, May 17, 2009, www.nytimes.com/2009/05/17/us/politics/17text-obama.html?pagewanted=all.

and Conservative Judaism and Modern Orthodox Judaism sought to distinguish themselves from both (and from each other); Baptists have been notably fissiparous over the centuries, as have the heirs of John Calvin in American Presbyterianism; the Anglican Communion's recent difficulties are familiar to all. Into none of these controversies, however, has the president of the United States ever injected himself and his office: until May of 2009, when President Obama did precisely that at Notre Dame. There, the president leapt into the middle of a decades-long ecclesiological debate within the Catholic Church in the United States by suggesting that the good Catholics—the real Catholics—were men like Fr. Theodore Hesburgh and the late Cardinal Joseph Bernardin, and indeed all those Catholics who supported the Obama candidacy in 2008 and agreed with the president on the nature of the common ground to be sought in American public life. President Obama, in other words, would be the arbiter of authentic Catholicism in America.

The Catholic Church can take care of itself, and is doing so in the face of this challenge. What I wish to underscore here is the gravity of the threat that the president's Notre Dame commencement address posed to the fabric of religious freedom in America—which is one constitutional expression of the third truth of the American Proposition and its understanding of the relationship of society and the state. The White House likely thought it was simply playing wedge politics, strengthening its grip on certain Catholic constituencies while driving a wedge between those Catholics and their bishops. But there was nothing simple about this. Here was the state, embodied by the president, claiming a purchase in what had for centuries been understood to be the inviolable territory of society. To be sure, President Obama is not the "Holy Roman Emperor Henry IV"; he is not contesting with the Pope for the legal authority to appoint bishops. But whether he knew he was doing this or not, the president in his Notre Dame address was usurping the bishops' right to define the doctrinal and moral boundaries of the Catholic community. That this astonishing act was not recognized for what it was is an important, and chilling, measure of the degree to which the third truth of the American Proposition is, at best, tenuously held these days.

Then there is the marriage debate. There is no need to rehearse this at length. Marriage is one of those societal institutions (like the parent-child bond) that antedate the state historically and are prior to the state ontologically and morally. It is not within the competence of the state to define marriage as the union of two men or two women, any more than it is within the state's competence to define marriage in polygamous or polyandrous terms. Any state that does so has breached the border between society and state in a way that gravely endangers civil society and the common good. Any state that does so is engaging in what Cardinal Joseph Ratzinger called, in his homily on April 18, 2005, the "dictatorship of relativism": the use of coercive state power to compel recognition of what is neither true nor good, in the name of a nihilist insouciance toward the true and a relativist concept of the good. Such dictatorships will, sooner or later, lead to what the late John Paul II described as "open or thinly disguised totalitarianism."[27]

As to the fourth truth within Murray's American Proposition—the truth that only a virtuous people can be free—the challenges from which it is under assault are so obvious as to need little exposition. Theories of democracy that reduce the democratic experiment to a matter of political mechanics chip away at the linkage between freedom and virtue by consigning virtue to the sphere of private life. The mantra of "choice," the unassailable trump in our contemporary public discourse, deliberately avoids the question of the good: Choose *what*? The reduction of public virtue to an ill-defined "tolerance" with no tether to what is objectively good erodes our sense that civil society is built on numerous virtues. The vulgarities of contemporary popular culture; the demeaning of women by a multibillion dollar pornography industry; the casual brutality of some aspects of our sports; the eroticism of so much advertising—all of these challenges to virtue are also challenges to freedom rightly understood. Decadence and democracy cannot indefinitely coexist. If the American experiment constantly requires new births of freedom, then the birth of freedom we need in the early twenty-first century is one in which freedom is once again tethered to both the true and the good.

Another Catholic Moment?

If the Catholic community in the United States did not, in the immediate aftermath of the Second Vatican Council and during the cultural whitewater of the Sixties, grasp the destiny that Murray envisioned for it, might it do so today?

Any such recovery of Catholic identity and Catholic nerve would have to address each of the defaults in America's loss of grip on the truths that constitute us as a unique and uniquely free people. The Church has been doing so for many decades now by insisting that the defense of the right to life of the unborn, and indeed of all innocent life from conception until natural death, is a first principle of justice that can be known by reason,

[27] Pope John Paul II, Encyclical Letter *Centesimus Annus* [Hundredth Year] (May 1, 1991), 46.

irrespective of one's theological "location" or lack thereof. More recently, the Church has taken up the cudgels of public argument in defense of marriage rightly understood, in defense of its own integrity as a self-governing institution, and in defense of the conscience rights of the people of the Church. These efforts must continue, and they must be intensified.

In addition, however, the Catholic Church in America, if it is to help rebuild the foundations of the American democratic experience in ordered freedom, must become evermore the Church that teaches America the truths about the principle of consent, and the priority of society over the state, as those truths are embodied in what modern Catholic social doctrine has called the principle of subsidiarity. According to this principle, the Church lifts up and honors those mediating institutions or voluntary associations that stand between the individual and the state, and teaches that decision making should be left as the lowest possible level of society—that is, the level of those most directly effected by the decision—commensurate with the common good.

These mediating institutions, and that rich pluralism of societal deliberation and decision making, constitute what John Paul II called the "subjectivity of society"; both the institutions and the pluralism are threatened today by the seemingly inexorable thrust of the modern state into every crevice of life.[28] Were the Church to take on this essential task of public moral education, some reconsideration of longstanding Catholic policy positions as articulated by the bishops of the United States might be required: How, for example, is it possible to achieve "universal" health insurance or health coverage while honoring the principle of subsidiarity? If the principle of subsidiarity is true, as we must affirm to be the case, then there must be answers to this question, and to related questions in the fields of education and social welfare. The search for those answers, which may well lie in a reconception of the roles of both government and "mediating institutions" in these fields, ought to help in the process of regrounding American public life in two of its foundational truths.[29]

The Choice Point

There has been welcome electoral evidence that what the advocates of the dictatorship of relativism imagined to have been their Waterloo-like rout

---

[28] On the "subjectivity of society," see Pope John Paul II, Encyclical Letter *Sollicitudo Rei Socialis* [Social Concerns] (December 30, 1987), 15.4, and *Centesimus Annus*, 13.2, 46.2.

[29] See Peter L. Berger and Richard John Neuhaus, *To Empower People: From State to Civil Society* (Washington, D.C.: American Enterprise Institute, 1995).

of the advocates of classical biblical morality and classical Western political philosophy in November 2008 was in fact no such thing. Yet Murray's template reminds us to be ever attentive to the deeper, long-term trends in our political culture. And over those same few months I have been struck by the number of thoughtful Americans who believe that we are living a defining moment in our national life: roads are indeed diverging in the wood, and the choices taken will have much to do with whether the United States at its tercentenary will be a political community in recognizable moral and cultural continuity with its founding. One more citation from Father Murray may help us grasp precisely what is at stake in the question of whether we still hold these truths:

> What is at stake is America's understanding of itself. Self-understanding is the necessary condition of a sense of self-identity and self-confidence, whether in the case of an individual or in the case of a people. If the American people can no longer base this sense on naïve assumptions of self-evidence, it is imperative that they find other more reasoned grounds for their essential affirmation that they are uniquely a people, uniquely a free people. Otherwise the peril is great. The complete loss of one's identity is, with all propriety of theological definition, hell. In diminished forms it is insanity. And it would not be well for the American giant to go lumbering about the world today, lost and mad.[30]

---

[30] Murray, *We Hold These Truths*, p. 18.

CHAPTER 8

Catholicism and the American Experiment

AMBASSADOR MICHAEL NOVAK
Ave Maria University

GEORGE WEIGEL has been the steadiest beacon of the thought of John Courtney Murray for many years. The brilliant essay in this volume is a much-deserved reminder of our debts to a giant who walked in our midst, showing us how to think of religious liberty—and of America—in a new way.

In the strong opening chapter in this volume by Cardinal George, to which Weigel is in effect responding, one major claim is that there are few or no cultural footholds for Catholicism to grab onto in order to take deep root in American soil. Cardinal George looks at Catholics rather more as strangers to American principles than Murray and Weigel do. The latter believe that "these truths we hold," as enunciated by the mostly Protestant Founders of America, are themselves deeply Catholic, rooted in the natural law, and derived from a biblical reading of liberty and community in history. In a way, Weigel and Murray both suggest Catholic philosophical and theological traditions actually give a fuller reading to "these truths" of the founding than many American Protestant traditions.

This is a subject worth thinking about: Is the American Experiment better understood in its richness in a Protestant or in a Catholic intellectual framework? Like Alexis de Tocqueville, Murray and Weigel do not quite assert, but plainly suggest, that Catholic ways of explaining the intellectual foundations of the American republic are in some ways deeper and richer than the Puritan traditions in which they were first articulated. In fact, Murray and Weigel set out to show just that, by way of friendly amendment and support.

Both Murray and Weigel are as strong and deep as is Cardinal George in identifying the soft nihilism hidden in some ways of defending the

American founding, ways which are in fact deadly to the survival of the Experiment. But more than Cardinal George, they allow for many more parallels, analogies, and connective tissues to Catholic ways of understanding. For example, they show links between the American Protestant emphasis on associations of all kinds, both ecclesiastical and civil, and the traditions of medieval associations and small communities.

The first law of democracy, Tocqueville roundly announced more than once, is the principle of association. And this principle thrived during the Catholic ages as it seldom has since, except in America.

Furthermore, in stressing the cultural distance between Catholic traditions and American culture, Cardinal George overlooks the difference between the many cultures of local America and the "superculture" imposed upon them during the last three generations by new media of national communication—cinema, radio, instantly drying ink on glossy pages (allowing for the triumph of national magazines in framing a national culture, in whose first ranks are a college-educated elite), and, last of all, huge, national television networks.

With this distinction in hand, one can easily see how the superculture is far more secular, even hostile to religion (or in its strongest form, more "Christophobic"), than America's local cultures. The languages spoken by ordinary Americans in their daily lives is far more religious, biblical, Christian—and more patriotic and flag-waving—than the language of the superculture. Indeed, even accents and word choices are different. Instantly on hearing her, many supercultural Americans rejected Sarah Palin with some disdain, and many other Americans recognized her as "one of us."

Indeed, one can make a plausible argument that the supercultural outlook is far removed from natural law and pro-life inclinations. By contrast, the local cultures of America, each in their differently accented ways, seem instantly more in harmony with a sense of the natural law, and in instinctive sympathy for life in the womb.

Next, to do an honest night's work, I should try to push Weigel's presentation of Murray's argument to a few new levels.

Like Weigel, I deeply appreciate Murray's emphasis on reason—he liked his reason as he liked his martinis, "desperately dry." But I have learned from Lonergan to sharpen and broaden my conception so as to include the intellectual skills required both for *insight* and for *judgment*. The latter require rather more attention to the five senses, to imagination, memory, moral sympathy, and the moral sense, than Murray's "desperately dry reason" connotes.

Second, although Murray is more sophisticated on matters of nature and grace than his critics such as David Schindler suggest, it remains true that Murray is not sufficiently guarded against seeming to rely on a "layer cake" view of nature and grace, as if the two were separate from each other. Murray was more sophisticated about Henri de Lubac, and discovered him far earlier, than Schindler thinks.

Third, as some of his students say of Leo Strauss, so of Murray it might be said that while he uncovered brilliant things about the philosophy of the American Founders, his own writings suffer from insufficient closeness to the texts of the Founders. Both Strauss and Murray, in different ways, choose a far more spare and lean set of quotations from the Founders, and ignore far too much rich and provocative material. The odd thing is that if they had given denser portraits of the thought of the Founders, in more exact detail, that very effort would have much strengthened their arguments. It would have forced them to admit, for instance, that other points they made about the Founders were less credible than they thought. The sharp line Strauss drew between the ancients and the moderns seems far too severe, for example—more Continental than Anglo-American.

Finally, I should end by also trying to stretch Murray's argument into new dimensions, not to contradict things he wrote, but to enlarge them. To the four "truths we hold" that Murray listed, I would propose three more. These lie masked but powerful in the statement of the first four.

The fifth truth we hold is that every human being sometimes sins. That is why it is necessary to design a republic that works in a society of sinners, with checks and balances and other precautions against the certain reality of frequent human sins. It is necessary to design a republic that works not only for saints but especially for sinners. There are so many more of the latter. (And the former are a bit hard to live with.)

The sixth truth is that the favorite form of reason used by the Founders was, not so much the formal, scholastic dryness that Murray tended to prefer, but rather common sense. Murray got closest to this when he used the term "prudence" rather than "logic" in describing the type of thought most useful and needed.

The seventh truth is that the primary American imperative is not, actually, the individual or the individual alone, but one or another form of community, as in the projects of uniting the *United* States, saving the *Union*, building *villages, cities, communities*, and *associations* of many sorts. Early Americans were proud to act as independent individuals, and to take up personal responsibilities. But in almost everything they have done, they have depended on union with others. The fundamental American reality is not the individual but the sort of virtuous *community* that nourishes strong and responsible individuals. Moreover, America's communities tend to nurture the kind of individuals who find fulfillment in "giving back" to their communities, and work hard to strengthen these communities for the future. For they want their children to share in the same blessings they did.

I thank George Weigel again for putting us all in his debt. In choosing to keep close to the center of his life the "Murray Project," he built better than he knew.

PART 3

Catholic Higher Education and Challenges in America

CHAPTER 9

Higher Education Vibrantly Catholic[1]

William Cardinal Levada
Prefect, Congregation for the Doctrine of the Faith

THIS IS the last Mass you will attend as undergraduates at Ave Maria University. In a few hours you will be on your way, with a carload of furniture and a heart full of memories, to begin a new and very different chapter of your life. The rhetoric for such occasions evokes predictable themes: the emotions of tearful farewells, pride and gratitude for achievements, excitement and apprehension about what lies ahead. It is also customary to look out at the world poised to greet you as you emerge onto its stage, diploma in hand. It is a world of great opportunities but tremendous economic insecurity, a global village that becomes smaller every day, it seems, with the breathtaking advances in social media, but a village that is plagued by terrorism, war, and social upheaval.

All of this is standard graduation fare, no less true for being so predictable. College students all across our nation are taking the step you take this morning. But as a graduate of Ave Maria University, there is another element to include in the mix, a characteristic which, while not unique to your school, is certainly professed and celebrated here with particular intensity: I refer, of course, to the vibrant Catholic identity of Ave Maria University. While Ave Maria has distinguished itself in many ways as a center of learning in just a few years, I suspect that a factor that weighed heavily in your decision to come here was the forthright Catholic ethos that shapes every aspect of this campus.

So, as you leave this oasis of Catholicity and go into the wider world, what might you expect, in terms of your Catholic faith? From a good many people, indifference. It is no secret that our country, although among the

[1] William Cardinal Levada, baccalaureate homily, Ave Maria University, May 7, 2011.

most religious in the developed world, is becoming increasingly secular. You will meet many people whom religion—any religion—simply does not touch in the least. Many of them will be good and generous people, but something which has been so integral to your life here, and, I hope, integral to you personally, will be beyond their experience. Furthermore, among those who do have an interest in religion, you will encounter a veritable marketplace of competing spiritualities. It has been said that the difference between France and the United States is that in France there are four religions and four hundred kinds of cheese, while in America we have four kinds of cheese and four hundred religions. The truth beneath that jest is that, from the earliest days of our nation, America has not only been a melting pot of cultures but a laboratory for religions. Finally, as a Catholic you will meet either suspicion or outright hostility from some people. This negativity has many sources, but this is not the occasion to dwell on them. Suffice it to say that if you don't know yet that a lot of people dislike the Catholic Church, you will know very soon.

And within the Church what do you find? A great deal of good, of course, of which this university is a wonderful example. But there is also a lot of polarization among Catholics on issues great and small. Tensions and disagreements are a part of life everywhere, and it would be naïve to expect the Church to be an exception to this, but there is a spirit of rancor and bitterness taking hold in some quarters, which can be very discouraging. We also acknowledge failures of leadership in the Church, as well as the ever-present reality of sin in the lives of all believers.

I offer this thumbnail sketch in the context of your graduation, but I also present it in the wider context of the Easter season. What I would like to suggest this morning is that your story has already been written, and we are reading it throughout this holy season in the Acts of the Apostles. When the first disciples left the Upper Room to carry the Gospel of Christ to the ends of the earth, their situation was similar to yours. They lived in the global village of the Roman Empire, a world linked by a system of roads that were the "information superhighway" of the ancient world. It was the era of the *Pax Romana*, but this peace was punctuated by the uprisings and terrorist attacks, and there was a great deal of political instability. For example, within a few years of Pentecost, the madman Caligula succeeded Tiberius as emperor, to be followed several years later by Nero. As those first disciples carried the Good News from place to place, their creed was viewed by many as simply one more curious oriental sect at the smorgasbord of religions on offer. Paul delivered a carefully crafted homily to the intelligentsia in Athens, only to be met with indifference. Rumors of immorality and sedition among Christians filled the first-century version of the blogs, prompting official persecution and informal disdain. And within the community? Heated arguments about how much of the inherited Jewish tradition must be maintained and how much accommodation to other cultures could be allowed threatened to tear the infant Church apart. As to failures in leadership, every time a disciple heard a rooster crow he had a reminder of that—at the root of it all, the scandal of a crucified Messiah.

What sustained the disciples in those first difficult years? Their intimacy with Christ. They had heard him teach; they had watched him perform miracles, feed the hungry, and heal the sick. They had seen him lay down his life on the Cross, and they ate and drank with him after he rose from the dead. This will sustain you, too, and it is Ave Maria's greatest gift to you: on this campus you have been privileged to live in the company of Jesus. You have heard him teach in your personal reading of the Scriptures and the proclamation of his Word in the liturgy. You have been fed by him in so many ways: through friends, through intellectual explorations enlightened by faith, [and] above all by the gift of his very Body and Blood in the Eucharist. You have been healed by him in the sacrament of reconciliation, where you have been privileged to hear him say to you what he said to poor sinners two thousand years ago: "Your sins are forgiven." You have stood at Calvary at every Mass, where his sacrifice becomes present, and, like the first disciples, you have recognized the Risen Jesus in the breaking of the bread. Truly our Lord can say to you what he said to his first followers: "Blessed are the eyes that see what you see. For I say to you, many prophets and kings desired to see what you see and did not see it, and to hear what you hear, but did not hear it" (Luke 10:23–24).

It is by staying close to Christ that we realize that God has chosen us in him before the foundation of the world, and by intimate communion with him we receive that new heart of which the prophet Ezekiel spoke. I urge you to retain and deepen the religious practices you have developed here. It is very likely that you will soon find yourselves in situations where the spiritual opportunities are not as convenient as they have been at Ave Maria. Time for personal prayer, participation in the sacramental life of the Church, an ongoing study of the truth of the faith will require a greater effort on your part. Make that effort, as the first disciples must have done when they found themselves far from the familiar surroundings of Galilee and Jerusalem. They knew that after the Resurrection Christ was even closer to them than he had been when they followed him from town to town, but that his presence needed to be attended to and nourished. Our friendship with Jesus Christ operates under [the] same laws of any other friendship: it demands time and energy. As Catholics, we have so many resources available to deepen that friendship, but we must not take it for granted.

While I exhort you to cherish the intimacy with Christ you have known here at Ave Maria, the fact is you are leaving. Peter could not stay on the mount of the Transfiguration, the disciples could not remain in the Upper Room, for one very simple reason: Christ is given to be shared, not simply kept. The great example of this is the patroness of your university. When Mary was graced with the greatest privilege accorded to any human being in history, to conceive and give birth to the Son of God himself, she might well have locked herself away in Nazareth to contemplate this tremendous mystery. Instead, we are told that she went in haste to her cousin Elizabeth to bring Christ to her and her unborn child. Now you must bring Christ to others. Your marching orders are implied in today's Gospel (Luke 10:21–24). Jesus says that no one knows the Father except the Son and anyone to whom the Son wishes to reveal him. That "anyone" is "everyone;" Christ wants no one to be excluded from the feast, and he has entrusted that invitation to you and to me.

This past Sunday [May 1, 2011] I had the great privilege of concelebrating holy Mass with Pope Benedict XVI, together with more than a million other pilgrims filling St. Peter's Square and the surrounding streets to participate in the beatification of the Servant of God Pope John Paul II. This great Pope, whom God gave as shepherd to guide his Church, just as the Risen Lord charged his predecessor St. Peter to "feed his sheep" out of love for him, was an apostle of hope. Blessed John Paul II lived in hope of a better world, convinced that he was called, just as all of us are called, to be architects of the "civilization of love."

I think of his challenge to the then communist rule in his native Poland and in Eastern Europe—of his inspiring confidence in young people, especially through the celebration of World Youth Days. I think too of his invitation to his fellow Christians to enter into dialogue with people of good will everywhere; of his Encyclical Letter *Fides et Ratio*, in which he outlined how faith and reason are partners in working toward the best that humanity can be.

In his homily Pope Benedict gave this beautiful testimony to his predecessor: "With his witness of faith, love, and apostolic courage, accompanied by his great human gifts, this exemplary son of the Polish nation helped Christians throughout the world not be afraid to call themselves Christian, to belong to the Church, to speak about the Gospel. In a word, he helped us not be afraid of the truth, because truth is the guarantee of [true] freedom."

Blessed John Paul left an enormous historical impact not only on the Church but also on the world. He was convinced that Jesus' commission to the apostles to bring the Gospel to the ends of the earth was meant to bring human history to its true fulfillment under the guidance of the Holy

Spirit. When I suggested earlier that the story of our lives has already been written and is read again by the whole Church in the Acts of the Apostles during the Easter season, I do not mean that in the sense of a replay of an old movie. The Acts of the Apostles is the first chapter of the history of how the mission of Christ began to unfold in the Church and in the world. But today's and tomorrow's chapters are ours to write—yours and mine—and for this reason we too have received the Pentecost gift of the Holy Spirit in the sacrament of confirmation.

Following the example of Blessed John Paul, Pope Benedict has returned to the importance of the dialogue of faith and reason in several of his most important addresses, for example between Muslims and Christians at the University of Regensburg, on the place of religion in a "lay" society, where church and state are separate; at the *College des Bernardins* in Paris; and more recently at Westminster Hall at the British Parliament. When he visited our country in 2008, the Holy Father also addressed the role of Christian witness in a secular society. Perhaps this excerpt from his remarks at Catholic University in Washington can serve as a valedictory challenge and guide to the 2011 graduating class of Ave Maria University:

> Secularism challenges the Church to reaffirm and to pursue more actively her mission in and to the world. As the Council made clear, the lay faithful have a particular responsibility in this regard. What is needed, I am convinced, is a greater sense of the intrinsic relationship between the Gospel and the natural law on the one hand, and, on the other, the pursuit of authentic human good, as embodied in civil law and in personal moral decisions. In a society that rightly values personal liberty, the Church needs to promote at every level of her teaching—in catechesis, preaching, seminary and university instruction—an apologetics aimed at affirming the truth of Christian revelation, the harmony of faith and reason, and a sound understanding of freedom, seen in positive terms as a liberation both from the limitations of sin and *for* an authentic and fulfilling life. In a word, the Gospel has to be preached and taught as an integral way of life, offering an attractive and true answer, intellectually and practically, to real human problems. The "dictatorship of relativism," in the end, is nothing less than a threat to genuine human freedom, which [can] only mature in generosity and fidelity to the truth.[2]

Your education at Ave Maria has equipped you well to follow the exhortation of St. Peter: "Always be ready to give an explanation to anyone

[2] Pope Benedict XVI, *Christ Our Hope: The Papal Addresses of the Apostolic Journey to the United States* (Mahwah, N.J.: Paulist Press, 2008), pp. 28–29.

who asks you for a reason for your hope" (1 Peter 3:15). This is an important part of the legacy of Ave Maria. Your school is a living response to an appeal made over a century ago by another Blessed recently raised to the altars, John Henry Newman, who said: "I want a laity, not arrogant, not rash in speech, not disputatious, but [people] who know their religion, who enter into it, who know just where they stand, who know what they hold and what they do not, who know their creed so well that they can give an account of it, who know so much of history that they can defend it."[3] The ability to know and defend the Catholic faith is an important part of the legacy of Ave Maria, but not the most important part. The most important part is the opportunity this school has afforded you to live with Christ and let him shape your life. The Church needs apologists, to be sure, but her greatest witness is found in the daily lives of conscientious Catholics. Blessed John Henry Newman touched on this point in a sermon delivered in his Anglican days. After describing the first disciples in one of his "parochial and plain sermons" he said:

> We, too, though we are not witnesses of Christ's actual resurrection, are so spiritually. By a heart awake from the dead, and by affections set on heaven, we can as truly witness that Christ liveth as they did. . . . He who obeys God conscientiously, and lives holily, forces all about him to believe and tremble before the unseen power of Christ. To the world indeed at large he witnesses not. . . . But to his neighbors he manifests the Truth in proportion to their knowledge of him; and some of them, through God's blessing, catch the holy flame, cherish it, and in turn transmit it. And thus in a dark world Truth still makes its way in spite of the darkness, passing from hand to hand.[4]

May it be said of each of you in the next chapter of your life that the better people come to know you, the more they know that Christ has risen! And may the Blessed Virgin Mary, patroness of Ave Maria University, guide her faculty, students, and alumni—and intercede for you all the days of your lives.

---

[3] John Henry Newman, *Present Position of Catholics in England* (London, 1851), pp. ix, 390.

[4] John Henry Newman, "Witnesses of the Resurrection," *Parochial and Plain Sermons*, vol. 1, sermon 22.

CHAPTER 10

Catholic Higher Education in America: Challenges and Prospects

THOMAS HIBBS
Dean of Honors College, Baylor University

IN A 1937 address to Catholic educators at the Midwest regional meeting of the National Catholic Education Association (NCEA), University of Chicago president Robert Hutchins issued what he termed a "scandalous accusation": "In my opinion . . . you have imitated the worst features of secular education and ignored most of the good ones." He went on to propose that the "best service Catholic education can perform for the nation and all education is to show that the intellectual tradition can again be made the heart of higher education."[1] For those who know the career and thought of Hutchins, perhaps the greatest public defender of liberal education in twentieth-century America, the statements are not surprising. What may be surprising, especially to those who have accepted the standard mainstream history of Catholic higher education in America, is the way these words are enthusiastically embraced—indeed

[1] Robert M. Hutchins, "The Integrating Principle of Catholic Higher Education," *College Newsletter*, Midwest Regional Unit, NCEA, May 1937, pp.1 and 4. See also Robert Hutchins, *The Higher Learning in America* (New Haven, CT: Yale University Press, 1936). Surveying the incoherence of the standard university curricula in America, Hutchins boldly proclaims "without theology or metaphysics a university cannot exist" (*The Higher Learning*, p. 99). The only type of unity evident in the modern university is that of an encyclopedia and its "alphabetical arrangement"; what is needed is a "hierarchy of truths" (ibid., p. 95). He calls for an "evangelistic movement" that would aim at the "conversion" of the individual and of the teaching profession itself to the "true conception of general education" (ibid., p. 87).

directly quoted—by John Tracy Ellis in his famous 1955 essay, "American Catholics and the Intellectual Life."[2]

Ellis's essay was both a lament of the current state of Catholic higher education and a hortatory statement of the need for Catholics to raise standards and expectations.[3] Alongside a plea for greater scholarly rigor in our universities, Ellis urged Catholic parents to inculcate habits of reading in their children. Because it focused on research and castigated Catholics for their ghetto mentality, the piece is often seen as initiating the process of secularization whose effects we can witness at those Catholic universities that have most enthusiastically embraced the research ideal of the great secular schools.[4] Indeed, the essay is sometimes envisioned as a first draft of the Land O' Lakes statement from the 1960s.[5] But it is nothing of the sort. Aside from the fact that there is no juridical element in the various theses Ellis propounds, the essay strikes, in its expressed hopes for American Catholic intellectual life, a distinctively countercultural note. With Tocqueville and Orestes Brownson, Ellis takes aim at the leveling features of American egalitarianism, at what Brownson called the "American practice of dethroning all distinctions." Even more striking is this passage:

> There is not a man of discernment anywhere today who is unaware that the intellectual climate of the United States is undergoing a radical change from the moribund philosophy of materialism and discredited liberalism that have ruled a good portion of the American mind for the better part of a century.[6]

---

[2] John Tracy Ellis, "American Catholics and the Intellectual Life," in *Thought* 30, Fall 1955: 351–88.

[3] For analogous analyses concerning the Evangelical world, see Carl F. H. Henry's *The Uneasy Conscience of American Fundamentalism* (Grand Rapids, Mich.: Eerdmans, 1949) and Mark Noll's *The Scandal of the Evangelical Mind* (Grand Rapids, Mich.: Eerdmans, 1994).

[4] The essay has also become part of the standard liberal narrative about conservatism and anti-intellectualism because it was quoted in a section of Richard Hofstadter's famous *Anti-Intellectualism in American Life*. For a balanced assessment that sees Ellis's essay as one of the sole attempts at uniting Catholic revivalism with assimilation, see Philip Gleason's *Contending with Modernity: Catholic Higher Education in the Twentieth Century* (New York, N.Y.: Oxford University Press, 1995), pp. 287–91, 322.

[5] The Land O' Lakes statement was issued by mostly Catholic educators and administrators in 1967 regarding the role and identity of Catholic universities. On this, see Gleason, *Contending with Modernity*, pp. 314–17.

[6] Ellis, "American Catholics," p. 387.

The danger for Catholics is that they will simply go with the flow. So, Ellis is critical both of a siege mentality and of conformity to the dominant cultural trends. These are of course the two great temptations for any immigrant population, especially one that had often suffered from virulent bigotry. Catholics combined a defensive stance with a longing for success as commonly understood in American society. It is easy from this perspective to see the way in which anti-intellectualism could become normative. The only significance of the intellectual life would be instrumental, in terms of its multiple utilities, especially for career advancement, professionalism, and apologetics.[7]

But generic scholarly excellence is not precisely what Ellis had in mind. In stark terms, Ellis describes one of the obstacles to Catholic academic excellence: self-betrayal. He writes:

> Part of the reason why American Catholics have not made a notable impression on the intellectual life of their country is due, I am convinced, to what might be called a betrayal of that which is peculiarly their own. The nature of that betrayal has been highlighted during the last quarter of a century by such movements as the scholastic revival in

[7] Ellis comments,

> While it is gratifying to learn that so many of the graduates of Catholic institutions pursue their studies beyond college by fitting themselves for the legal and medical professions, it is to be regretted that a proportionately high number do not manifest a like desire, or find a similarly strong stimulation, to become trained scholars in the fields where the Catholic tradition of learning is the strongest (ibid., p. 360).

Furthermore, he observes, "More damaging than its direct effect on the intellectual shortcomings of American Catholics, has probably been the fostering by this historic bias of an overeagerness in Catholic circles for apologetics rather than pure scholarship" (ibid., p. 361). Initially Ellis cites anti-Catholic bias as a source of Catholic underachievement. But then toward the end he dismisses that excuse and argues that really lack of industry has been the chief problem. He writes,

> But who, one may rightly ask, has been responsible in the main for its inadequacy? Certainly not the Church's enemies, for if one were to reason on that basis St. Augustine would never have written the *City of God*, St. Robert Bellarmine the *Tractatus de potestate summi pontificis*, nor would Cardinal Baronius have produced the *Annales ecclesiastici*. In fact, it has been enmity and opposition that have called forth some of the greatest monuments to Catholic scholarship (ibid., p. 361).

From this list of what are simultaneously great works of scholarship and polemics, it is clear that mere assimilation to secular standards is not what Ellis has in mind for Catholic scholarship.

> philosophy which found its most enthusiastic and hard-working friends on the campuses of the University of Chicago, the University of Virginia, Princeton University, and St. John's College, Annapolis. Meanwhile the Catholic universities were engrossed in their mad pursuit of every passing fancy that crossed the American educational scene, and found relatively little time for distinguished contributions to scholastic philosophy. Woefully, lacking in the endowment, training, and equipment to make them successful competitors of the secular universities in fields like engineering, business administration, nursing education, and the like, the Catholic universities, nonetheless, went on multiplying these units and spreading their budgets so thin—in an attempt to include everything—that the subjects in which they could, and should, make a unique contribution were sorely neglected.[8]

There is a lot in this passage, part of which could apply to some of those Catholic universities that have escaped the Catholic ghetto, achieved widespread scholarly recognition, but in the process have become multiversities and neglected distinctively Catholic areas of research. The list of schools at which, according to Ellis, scholasticism has found "enthusiastic and hard-working friends" is intriguing, especially the inclusion of St. John's College. St. John's and its famous great books program were offshoots of the Hutchins project at the University of Chicago.[9] Chicago and St. John's inspired some of the earliest attempts at integrated, primary text liberal education in Catholic institutions. The Chicago program influenced the University of Notre Dame's Program of Liberal Studies, whose first incarnation was in the law school,[10] while the St. John's model was adopted at the Integrated Program at St. Mary's College, which in turn spawned Thomas Aquinas College. It is striking that the curricular impact here runs in one direction from secular to Catholic, but the intellectual influence is reciprocal. Partly through the influence of his friend and colleague, Mortimer Adler, Hutchins developed a conception of the goal of

[8] Ibid., p. 374.

[9] The Hutchins project is often misunderstood as an attempt to impose a great books curriculum upon an entire university. Instead, it was an attempt to create a true intellectual community. "By posing fundamental questions about the aims of education and the purposes of the university, he kept the campus in turmoil, and this differentiated *Hutchins' University, 1929–1951*, from other institutions of higher learning more sharply than has since been the case" (William H. McNeill, *Hutchins' University: A Memoir of the University of Chicago, 1929–1950* [Chicago: University of Chicago Press, 2007], p. viii).

[10] See Nicholas Ayo, Michael Crowe, and Julia Marvin, eds., *The First Fifty Years*, Program of Liberal Studies, University of Notre Dame, accessed December 13, 2011, pls.nd.edu/about/history/documents/PLS_History.pdf.

education as formation in intellectual virtue, a conception decisively informed by the writings of Newman and St. Thomas.[11]

Other examples of the curricular influence could be cited. For example, a miniversion of a great books program continues to flourish at Boston College, under the title Perspectives, whose curriculum is largely due to the vision of Ernest Fortin and his friendship with yet another Chicago faculty member, Allan Bloom. Yet, the Chicago project was not the first. Columbia's general education curriculum, which began in 1919 and flourished under the leadership of John Erskine, has been dubbed "the most famous course ever in the history of American curriculum."[12] These programs appealed to dedicated Catholic educations not for any restorationist reasons, as if they ever wished to restore the Middle Ages, but because they indicated how there are wisdom traditions in the past that have important insights for faculty and students facing the problems of fragmentation and dehumanization in contemporary cultures.

One of the students who profited from Columbia's curricular innovations and the faculty who formed its distinctive culture was a young Thomas Merton. When Merton began his studies at Columbia in 1935, he found himself in an English literature course taught by Mark Van Doren, whose pedagogy had a transformative impact on Merton: "Who is this man who really loves what he has to teach, and does not secretly detest all literature, and abhor poetry, while pretending to be a professor of it?"[13] Merton was drawn to the course because it addressed the most important questions

---

[11] See Hutchins, *Higher Learning*, pp. 63–68.

[12] W. B. Carnochan, *The Battleground of the Curriculum* (Stanford, Calif.: Stanford University Press, 1993), p. 71. Carman put it even more directly. "In introducing the general survey course," he said, "Columbia has operated on the assumption that it is not the fundamental business of the College to turn out specialists in a narrow field, and that an individual is, after all, not well educated unless he or she has at least some conception of the broad field of intellectual endeavor" (Harry J. Carman, "The Columbia Course in Contemporary Civilization," an address delivered before the Association of History Teachers of the Middle States and Maryland at Bryn Mawr, May 2, 1925 [published as a booklet by the Columbia College dean], p. 2). The goal of a Columbia education, Carman continued, was not to guide students into careers but "to help them see life broadly" (p. 3). Erskine traced the genesis of his course to a widespread concern within the faculty about "the literary ignorance of the younger generation." In particular, many faculty believed that students rarely, if ever, read truly classic texts: "the Bible, or Homer, or Vergil, or Dante, or the other giants whom the world at large have long esteemed" (John Erskine, *My Life as a Teacher* [Philadelphia and New York: J. B. Lippincott, 1948], p. 165).

[13] Thomas Merton, *The Seven Storey Mountain* (New York: Harcourt Brace, 1948), p. 141.

and spoke to the deepest longings of the human soul, and it did so in a way that crossed standard disciplinary divisions into literature, philosophy, and theology: "It was the only place where I ever heard anything really sensible about any of the things that were really fundamental—life, death, time, love, sorrow, fear, wisdom, suffering, eternity."[14] It is also at Columbia that Merton would encounter a group of students with a passion for books, with a love of conversation, and with a commitment to probing the most important questions about their lives. It was here that he became familiar with the writings of Maritain, Gilson, St. Thomas, and a host of medieval authors, who were being read enthusiastically by faculty and students alike.

In what Merton has to say about his time at Columbia, we can discern certain key elements of a truly liberal education. First, it should respond to the most important questions of human life, questions posed at least implicitly by all human beings at one time or another. Second, this sort of education understands itself as responding to a felt need, a lack, a longing in the soul. Third, it should reflect and help students to reflect upon the relationship of the parts of their education to one another and to the unified whole and end of the curriculum. Fourth, it should embody and cultivate a community of inquirers in which faculty converse with one another and with students, and students converse with one another both inside and outside the classroom.

Much of what Merton found at Columbia is woefully lacking in our contemporary research universities. In his recent book, *God, Philosophy, and Universities*, Alasdair MacIntyre argues "neither the university nor philosophy is any longer seen as engaging the questions" of "plain persons." These questions include: "What is our place in the order of things? Of what powers in the natural and social world do we need to take account? How should we respond to the facts of suffering and death? What is our relationship to the dead? What is it to live a human life well? What is it to live it badly?"[15]

The university is silent about the fundamental questions of human life, even as its administrators issue "stuttering ineptitudes" concerning the relationships of means to end and part to whole. MacIntyre writes, "In contemporary American universities each academic discipline is treated as autonomous and self-defining, so that its practitioners, or at least the most prestigious and influential among them, prescribe to those entering the discipline what its scope and limits are. And in order to excel in any one particular discipline, one need in general know little or nothing about any of the others." That raises the question,

[14] Ibid., p. 178.

[15] Alasdair MacIntyre, *God, Philosophy, Universities: A Selective History of the Catholic Philosophical Tradition* (Lanham, N. Dak.: Rowman and Littlefield, 2009), p. 9.

To whom then in such a university falls the task of integrating the various disciplines, of considering the bearing of each on the others, and of asking how each contributes to the overall understanding of the nature and order of things? The answer is 'No one,' but even that answer is misleading. For there is no sense in the contemporary American university that there is such a task, that something that matters is being left undone."[16]

About the last point MacIntyre seems simply wrong. In the early twenty-first century, in America's elite universities, institutions renowned across the globe, there is growing unease. Having become increasingly skeptical about knowledge itself, our most prestigious educational institutions now find themselves ill equipped to educate youth for the common good—or so an emerging consensus would have us believe.

Criticism of higher education is nothing new; among conservatives, it constitutes a sport that never seems to go out of season. Yet, in recent years, criticism has arisen from within mainstream liberal academia. Two books from Harvard administrators are signs of this spirit of self-criticism. Derek Bok, former president at Harvard, has written *Our Underachieving Colleges*; and Harry Lewis, a former dean at Harvard, has just published *Excellence without a Soul: How a Great University Forgot Education*—a central contention of which is the dismal judgment that the "ideal of liberal education lives on in name only."[17] (One would need to add to these, books by Anthony Kronman, former head of Yale law school; a forthcoming book and numerous essays by Andrew Delbanco of Columbia; and essays by *New York Times* columnist David Brooks.)[18] The complaints for which Allan Bloom was once reviled are now common in higher education. Many are now pondering Hutchins's question from the 1930s: Why is it that the "chief characteristic of higher learning is its disorder"?[19]

The failure of elite universities to deliver on their core mission is the lament running through Harry Lewis's *Excellence without a Soul.* With a

[16] Ibid., pp. 15–16.

[17] Derek Bok, *Our Underachieving Colleges* (Princeton, N.J.: Princeton University Press, 2006); Harry Lewis, *Education without a Soul: How a Great University Forgot Education* (New York: PublicAffairs, 2007), p. 13.

[18] Anthony Kronman, *Education's End: Why Our Colleges and Universities Have Given Up on the Meaning of Life* (New Haven, Conn.: Yale University Press, 2007); see the interview with Delbanco on his forthcoming book: "The State of Liberal Education," in *The Cresset* LXXIV, no. 1 (2008), pp. 6–12. For Brooks, see "The Organization Kid," *The Atlantic Monthly*, April, 2001.

[19] Hutchins, *Higher Learning*, p. 94. Some of the objections involve old-fashioned moral critique. In much less detached prose, Tom Wolfe's last novel, *I Am Charlotte Simmons*, released in 2004, depicted undergraduates at an elite university

curriculum void of coherence and faculty lacking a sense of teaching as a noble calling, students find that education offers no sense of "larger purpose in life." The libertarianism of the faculty who want to be left alone to do their research complements the laissez-faire attitude of students. Instead of being "immersed in the life of the mind," students act like the good consumers universities increasingly conceive them to be—maximizing upscale pleasures and opportunities for career advancement. Calls for reform, of which Lewis's book is but the latest in a long list, must overcome the vested interests of both students and faculty, who have an unspoken agreement about their own freedom. The laissez-faire attitude of the precocious teenager meets the professional libertarianism of the faculty. Mr. Lewis is not the first to wonder whether the turning of students into consumers is to the clear detriment of the ideals of liberal education.

In this atmosphere, universities can easily lose track of the one thing necessary for a university, the one thing that it alone can foster: the cultivation of the intellect. As Lewis notes, what is distinctive about college life is the possibility it offers students for a short but crucial period in the years between adolescence and adulthood to become "immersed in the life of the mind." College is freedom *for*, not freedom *from*.

In his classic *The Idea of a University*, John Henry Newman argues that liberal education can be justified only if "knowledge is capable of being its own end."[20] Although Newman defended professional training, he argued forcefully that universities ought to develop in students a philosophical habit of mind, a habit of wonder and an ability to trace the relationships among different parts of knowledge. One of the reasons for the inclusion of all branches of knowledge in the university curriculum is that even though students "cannot pursue every subject, they will still gain from living among those who represent the whole circle."[21]

There are manifold obstacles to realizing Newman's idea in today's university. Given the increasing emphasis on specialization in faculty research, few if any faculty can be said even to approximate representing the "whole circle." And of course students do not "live among" the faculty anyhow.

(Mr. Wolfe called the place Dupont University, but rumors abounded that his target was Duke) as booze-saturated, athlete-worshipping, sexual libertines. Reviewers, particularly from the academic world, were less than generous. But, if we are to believe *Rolling Stone* magazine's stunning expose, "Sex at Duke: Raging Parties, Random Hookups & the Girls Who Say the Lacrosse Players Aren't Guilty," Mr. Wolfe's book is a fairly accurate description of drinking and mating habits in the elite social world of schools like Duke.

20 John Henry Newman, *The Idea of a University* (Notre Dame: University of Notre Dame Press, 1982), p. 77.

21 Ibid., p. 76.

The shared libertarianism of faculty and students results in a diminishing number of contact hours between students and faculty, and even between faculty, who rarely know colleagues outside their own department.

Specialization breeds an inevitable individualism and elevates narrow expertise over breadth of learning. Clearly a university cannot do without rigorous, specialized knowledge in its faculty. The challenge Mr. Lewis and others pose is whether universities can create incentives to balance focus with breadth. This would entail another sense of liberalism. Such a liberality or generosity of spirit would revive a proper appreciation of amateurism—not in the sense of an absence of serious training but in the etymological meaning of the word "amateur," from the French for "lover."

In an academic context, an amateur would be one who has a passionate enthusiasm for knowledge, an infectious joy at human inquiry itself, and a commitment to transforming students from dependent absorbers of information into colleagues in a shared pursuit of knowledge. This spirit of wonder is the most compelling embodiment of Newman's claim that knowledge is an end in itself. Such a spirit knows no bounds—it can be equally present in an English poetry class, a chemistry lab, a music tutorial, or a philosophy seminar.

The defense of liberal education as both invigorating for young souls and an indirect catalyst for social transformation stretches from Socrates to W. E. B. DuBois, who in his famous *The Souls of Black Folk* penned the most eloquent defense of liberal education ever composed by an American. DuBois is best known for his debate with Booker T. Washington over post-Reconstruction civil rights strategies. A consequence of Washington's more conservative approach is the continued exclusion of African-Americans from higher education.

Although ignored in contemporary retellings of this standoff, DuBois makes higher education the centerpiece of his argument. For DuBois, this was about more than simply equal opportunity. To refuse African-Americans access to a truly liberal education, to relegate them to training in trades, was to deny their full humanity. Every other sort of education renders human beings fit to perform this or that role in business or society; it makes them serviceable, as we say. But this is to treat education—and human beings—in a merely instrumental fashion.

DuBois shares Socrates's objections to a citizenry that gives no thought to true education, to the state of the soul, to pondering what DuBois calls the "riddle of existence."[22] DuBois asserts, "[T]he true college will ever have one goal—not to earn meat, but to know the end and aim of that life which meat nourishes."[23] In response to the statement of the god at Delphi,

22 W. E. B. DuBois, *The Souls of Black Folk*, with an introduction by Henry Louis Gates Jr. (New York: Bantam Classic, 1989), p. 58.

23 Ibid.

Socrates asks, "Whatever does the god mean? What is his riddle?"[24] This is precisely the language DuBois uses in his eloquent description of the nature of true education.

> The riddle of existence is the college curriculum that was laid before the Pharoahs, that was taught in groves by Plato, that formed the trivium and quadrivium, and is to-day laid before the freedman's sons by Atlanta University. And this course of study will not change; its methods will grow more deft and effectual, its content richer by toil of scholar and sight of seer; but the true college will ever have one goal—not to earn meat, but to know the end and aim of that life which meat nourishes.[25]

Calling to mind Socrates's persistent comparison of the true educator to the experts who train individuals in crafts, DuBois writes, "The final product of our training must be neither a psychologist nor a brickmason, but a man. And to make men, we must have ideals, broad, pure, and inspiring ends of living,—not sordid money getting, not apples of gold."[26]

Losing track of its primary goal, higher education lapses into the sort of confused state Mr. Lewis describes, and fosters in students the sense that they are nothing more than hollow consumers for whom success is a well-padded resume. DuBois was confident that a truly liberal education could be truly liberating, that it could provide a counter to the instrumentalism that threatens to crowd out an appreciation of life's larger purposes.

The accusation that Socrates leveled against Athens is quite applicable to contemporary America: "You are an Athenian, a citizen of the greatest city with the greatest reputation for both wisdom and power; are you not ashamed of your eagerness to possess as much wealth, reputation, and honors as possible, while you do not care nor give thought to wisdom or truth, or the best possible state of your soul?"[27] In the course of his trial, Socrates poses this challenge to his fellow citizens. For the first of all the great philosophers in the Western tradition, the "care of the soul"—the pursuit of knowledge and virtue—is the chief task imposed on us as rational human beings.

Another way to express DuBois's argument is to say that he, like Socrates, takes the term "soul" seriously, as indicating a sense of what is higher and lower, better and worse, in human life. The word "soul" also

---

[24] Plato, *Apology* 21b.

[25] DuBois, *Souls*, p. 58.

[26] Ibid., p. 61.

[27] Plato, *Apology*, trans. G. M. A. Grube (Indianapolis, Ind.: Hackett Publishing, 1981), 29E.

figures in the title of Lewis's book about Harvard. But what does Lewis mean by "soul"? Can contemporary academics use the term without putting it in scare quotes to indicate its status as a relic from a bygone age of religious primitivism? Without snickering, can we seriously pose to our students the challenge Socrates posed to the Athenians, who in this case are a pretty good stand-in for Americans? Can we issue the challenge to give more care to the soul than to the body? If that is right, then the problems facing the modern university in its attempt to recover its liberal arts mission go much deeper and may be more intractable than any of its contemporary critics have thus far acknowledged.

It may well be that classical liberal education presupposes and embodies a distinctive philosophical and theological anthropology or at least that it must see itself as an attempt to answer the question, what does it mean to be a human being?[28] Might it be that forgetfulness of soul is the source of what Hutchins identifies as the chief characteristic of the higher learning in our time, namely, disorder? MacIntyre's book on God, philosophy, and the universities has in fact very little to say about universities; yet a thesis about human nature and the loss of the Aristotelian and Thomist language, soul and body quietly permeates the book. At the center of a Catholic university would be the articulation and dialectical development of the Catholic account of human nature. MacIntyre writes, "Such an account will have to integrate what we can learn about the nature and constitution of human beings from physicists, chemists, and biologists, historians, economists, and sociologists, with the kind of understanding of human beings that only theology can afford."[29] Philosophy, on this view, is required not only to articulate the Catholic understanding of nature and human nature but also to bring that understanding into conversation and debate with the conceptions of human nature, often only implicit, in the natural and social sciences. It also needs to be involved in ongoing dialogue with ancient, medieval, and modern rival philosophical understandings of human nature.

Something like this conversation and debate needs to occur with respect to the university and the nature of higher learning as well. We certainly need to think, along with authors such as Newman, of different conditions and distinctive visions of Catholic education in particular institutions. Indeed, diversity in higher education is our friend. As Francis Oakley, in one of the few recent books that paints a fairly optimistic picture of higher education, puts it, one of the great strengths of American higher education is the diversity of its institutions and the entrepreneurial

---

[28] See MacIntyre, *God, Philosophy, Universities*, p. 177 and throughout.

[29] Ibid., p. 177.

spirit that drives the creation of new schools.[30] Diversity exists not just between colleges and universities, secular and religious schools, or Protestant and Catholic institutions. It also exists within each of these groups and thus within Catholic institutions. We should welcome variety here. We can and should have arguments about better and worse, but we ought also to realize that no school can do everything well. Indeed, there is a certain contingency involved in the very foundations of institutions, a confluence of unpredictable and often unrepeatable events that contribute to the peculiar vision of a college or university. Consider the unusual alliance in the founding of the University of Dallas of Hungarian Cistercians and figures involved in the Southern literary renaissance, or the unusual combination in the origins of Thomas Aquinas College of individuals who had been trained both at Laval and in the integrated program at St. Mary's.

Diversity in pedagogical vision is likely to result not only from these sorts of contingent influences at the moment of founding but also from the universal need of every contemporary American Catholic college and university to respond to a question to which there is no obvious answer. We have it on good authority that the young cannot profitably study subjects like moral philosophy or metaphysics.[31] As Aristotle puts it in *Rhetoric*,

> While young men become geometricians and mathematicians and wise in matters like these, it is thought that a young man of practical wisdom cannot be found. The cause is that such wisdom is concerned not only with universals but with particulars, which become familiar from experience, but a young man has no experience. . . . One might ask this question too, why a boy may become a mathematician, but not a philosopher or a physicist. It is because the objects of mathematics exist by abstraction, while the first principles of these other subjects come from experience, and because young men have no conviction about the latter, but merely use the proper language, while the essence of mathematical objects is plain enough to them.[32]

---

30 Francis Oakley, *Community of Learning: The American College and the Liberal Arts Tradition* (New York: Oxford University Press, 1992).

31 On this, see Etienne Gilson, *Thomas Aquinas and Our Colleagues* (Princeton, N.J.: Princeton University Press, 1953), reprinted in *A Gilson Reader*, edited with an introduction by Anton Pegis (New York: Doubleday, 1957), pp. 278–97, and Ernest Fortin, "The Paradoxes of Aristotle's Theory of Education," in *The Birth of Philosophical Christianity* (Lanjam, Md.: Rowman and Littlefield, 1996), pp. 209–22.

32 Aristotle, *Rhetoric* 2.14.1390b9.

Thus, it is not immediately clear precisely what sort of education we ought to offer American eighteen-year-olds.[33] Indeed, the answer to this question will determine to some extent the structure of the curriculum.

What is clear is that the beginning of this education will be a protreptic in the classical sense, an introductory turning of the soul to the most important things. Thus, it will be an introduction that is more than a matter of rudimentary skills in writing, logic, and other ancillary disciplines. Rather we need a protreptic that awakens in students a sense of their own lack, their need. They need to become aware that they do not know, and they need to have their desire for the intellectual life inflamed. We need a protreptic in intellectual eros—insisting with students that they are heirs of a great tradition of learning that they could delightfully spend the rest of their lives trying to master and barely make a beginning, and immersing them in a sense of the whole, in which they must be active participants and of which they must be rigorous interpreters. This may involve not just learning but, as Augustine indicates of the philosophical schools of antiquity, unlearning as a prelude to learning. The meaning of education is to be led forth; now, the obstacles to a proper understanding of education can be either conservative or liberal. Understanding the structure of human life as a quest and the university as the arena for an intellectual quest presupposes a conception of human agency as pitched between presumption and despair, peremptory certitude and paralyzing doubt.

The quest in and of the university is a search for truth. In a book published not long before he died, *Truth and Truthfulness*, the stridently secular British philosopher Bernard Williams noted that we live in a time when the demand for truth has never been greater.[34] But, he added, we have never been more doubtful about our ability to reach the truth or even whether there is truth to be had. Williams saw the cultural, and particularly academic, despair over truth as a troubling sign. He criticized the ironic distance from which many academics, particularly in the humanities, approached *truth*. If we lose our hold on the truth, he observed, we risk losing everything. Both Pope John Paul II and Pope Benedict XVI would concur. Their recalling of the Church's universities to a recovery of their Catholicity is simultaneously a reminder of what makes them universities.

We might put this point in terms of a distinction borrowed from Alasdair MacIntyre between goods internal and external to a practice. Internal

---

[33] See also *Nicomachean Ethics* 6.9.1142a12–20 and the *Politics* 7.15.1334b26–27: "Care of the soul should be preceded by that of the body, which must be followed immediately by training of the appetites."

[34] Bernard Williams, *Truth and Truthfulness* (Princeton, N.J.: Princeton University Press, 2004).

goods are constitutive of the practice itself; without them, the practice could no longer exist or at least could not exist in the same form. External goods are extrinsic to the practice itself but may be closely allied to it as consequences. The problem with modern education is that it is far too beholden to the external goods. Socrates, Newman, Hutchins, and DuBois concur in the judgment that instrumentalization is the great enemy of a truly liberal education.[35] In MacIntyre's terms, this is to treat the internal goods of education, the chief of which is truth itself, as a means to other goods. We like to focus on careerism or the reduction to preprofessional education. But instrumentalization can occur when the chief role of education is expressed in political terms as preparation for citizenship, whether that is construed in a classical republican way or in a trendy liberal way.[36] Education can also be instrumentalized with respect to religion and then it can easily degenerate into apologetics, catechesis, or training in habits of devotion.

In defending, as we should, the notion that knowledge is its own end, that wonder is proper to human nature, we ought to be careful not to obscure the link between the good and the useful. Newman was careful to avoid this—so was DuBois. Newman found a place for professional education in his university and noted that what is desirable for its own sake can only be productive of other goods. The good, as Dionysius puts it in a line much beloved by medieval thinkers, is diffusive.[37] DuBois, for his part, insists that the goal of education is "not to inspire human hearts with a vision of the true, the good, and beautiful without pointing the practical way of realizing some of these dreams here and now in their own lives."[38] Education, he argues, must balance ideals with the "greater need of special-

[35] For a quite different defense of the goods intrinsic to university education and an excoriation of the practice of politicizing the curriculum, see Stanley Fish, *Save the World on Your Own Time* (New York: Oxford University Press, 2008).

[36] The vast majority of black Americans, as of white, will devote themselves to technical education, not liberal education. For all of DuBois's emphasis on the intrinsic desirability of liberal education, he does not hesitate to speak of its practical, political, and social ramifications. One of his chief arguments against Washington's willingness to limit education to the rudiments of knowledge followed by specialized training in a trade is that it leaves out of account the question who will teach the teachers, who will teach them how to understand their own work in relation to the whole of learning. Another argument concerns education as preparation for virtuous citizenship: "No secure civilization can be built in the south with the Negro as an ignorant, turbulent proletariat" (DuBois, *Souls*, p. 73).

[37] In this context, Stanley Rosen's reading of Plato in terms of a theoretico-productive conception of the intellect is pertinent. See my article "Modern Ancients: Stanley Rosen's Achievement," in the *Weekly Standard*, November 25, 2002.

[38] DuBois, *Souls*, p. 73.

ization and technique." Knowledge is intrinsically desirable; the anti-instrumental conception of knowledge and education does not mean that the knowledge is useless in the pejorative sense. Indeed, DuBois's statement that education investigates the "end and aim of that life which meat nourishes" indicates that it is eminently practical. It informs how we ought to live; it is, in Platonic language, an inquiry into the good. Or, in the language DuBois himself uses to describe St. Francis's account of education, it helps to satisfy the greater wants of the human soul, for "human service and sympathy," for "knowledge and inspiration," for "hope and truth and beauty."

To recover the rich connections between the good and the useful, we need to rescue the properly Catholic understanding of vocation from its degraded contemporary substitute, vocationalism. We might also turn to the classic Thomistic understanding of the good life as the mixed life, the life wherein contemplation overflows into action: *contemplata allis tradere* (hand on to others the fruit of our contemplation).[39] There is, further, a need to think about the proper role of industry and entrepreneurial spirit in the life of the university. One cannot help but be struck by Ellis's description of non-Catholic schools in which there are "enthusiastic and hard-working friends" of Catholic thought. Ellis is clearly appalled at the sheer laziness of many of his contemporary academics. But how should we construe the role of the entrepreneur in Catholic education? No, I am not thinking mainly of fundraising or of whether we ought to have business schools. And I am not thinking of the increasing tendency to construe students as consumers, something that presupposes that they already know what they want and that their thought and desire do not need shaping by the very education they seek.

At least in one respect, parents and potential students need to use the market to their advantage. They need to be better consumers, tougher negotiators, and refuse to follow the herd of parents who mindlessly rattle off a list of acceptable schools. The converse of the truth concerning competition among students for admission to selective schools is that schools compete very hard to lure good students. They need to be forced to compete even harder. The consumer element is not entirely inapplicable. Furthermore, we need more faculty, staff, and administrators with something of an entrepreneurial spirit, with a passion not just for scholarship and teaching but for building a certain kind of institution.

---

[39] Those of us devoted to Josef Pieper's book *Leisure, the Basis of Culture* and its denigration of work might want to consult Yves Simon's gentle critique of that book in his *Work, Society and Culture* (New York: Fordham University Press, 1971), in which he argues that the "good worker and the lover of truth have much in common" (p. 187).

One of the great complaints about contemporary education is the lack of integration. Of course, if you are allergic to saying what the ends of education are, you will likely have trouble saying how the parts fit together. Newman has not only a classical sense of ends and of the part-whole relationship but a supple account of what we might call cognitive development, an account that lends itself to, and might provide a corrective to the weaknesses in, contemporary interest in interdisciplinary curricula. As John Henry Newman states in *Idea of a University*,

> We know, not by a direct and simple vision, not at a glance, but, as it were, by piecemeal and accumulation, by a mental process, by going round an object, by the comparison, the combination, the mutual correction, the continual adaptation, of many partial notions, by the employment, concentration, and joint action of many faculties and exercises of mind. Such a union and concert of the intellectual powers, such an enlargement and development, such a comprehensiveness, is necessarily a matter of training . . . of discipline and habit.[40]

Enlargement, development, adaptation, and the habituation of the intellect in the discernment of the integrated complexity of the objects of knowledge—all this is proper to the human intellect and the proper object of a truly liberal education. Of course, there are all sorts of objections to interdisciplinary education, and it is easy to do a superficial job at it. But then it is easy to do a superficial job in discipline-specific education as well. The biggest obstacles to interdisciplinary education are the vested interests of departments and the increasingly narrow conception of research.

Some will say that there are many ways in which such universities can be Catholic apart from hiring Catholics to teach. That is not so clear, however, when the trend is toward a contraction of the broad scope and the rich tradition of Catholic liberal education to issues of social justice and service, issues to which secular schools can be equally devoted. In addition to contraction, there is marginalization, as the Catholic elements are relegated to campus ministry or specialized Catholic centers, sometimes even centers for Catholic studies. But a state university open to the serious study of religion could, according to these criteria, be equally "Catholic."

Another little explored element in Newman that is germane to our current situation has to do with his belief that students ought to live among those who have had an experience of the whole circuit of knowledge. Newman clearly has in mind here a collegiate rather than a university model. But this points us to an underappreciated or, to be more

---

[40] DuBois, *Souls*, p. 59, quoting from Newman, *Idea of a University*, pp. 114–15.

precise, misunderstood component of the university: student life. Certainly if *student life*, encompassing what happens on campus but outside the classroom, fosters habits of self-indulgence, moral relativism, and anti-intellectualism, then it will matter very little what goes on in the classroom. But curbing the sort of collegiate bacchanalian reverie depicted in Tom Wolfe's novel *I Am Charlotte Simmons* is not the only or the primary goal of Catholic office of student life. We need in fact to eliminate the term "dormitory," places where students retreat to sleep (or not), from our vocabulary. There is a huge opportunity here for partnerships between student life and the academic units of the university, the goal of which would be to integrate academic and student life, what goes on in the classroom and what occurs in the dorm. The purpose is to raise the level of conversation both inside and outside the classroom and thus to create a true community of learning.

Along with the hiring of faculty and the curriculum, student life is one of the three indispensable elements of a university. Catholic universities should be able to say how student life operates in a distinctively Catholic manner. If a Catholic institution cannot say how these three elements are distinctively Catholic and if it cannot say how they are interconnected, then students will not glimpse the Catholic conception of the unity of truth or the compatibility of faith and reason. Indeed, parents wondering exactly how Catholic a school is should ask—not only about hiring and curriculum—but also about the liturgical life of students and even the number of vocations the school produces.

One has the sense that many discussions of the religious identity of Catholic universities perform the same function as our endless national conversation about education reform: they effectively insulate the institution from any real change. One sometimes hears that there is no real cause for concern: Catholic universities will not go the way of the great Protestant universities, because Catholic institutions have a different understanding of faith and reason. However, if almost no one on the faculty or in the administration can articulate that difference, it is difficult to see how that understanding will ensure the perpetuation of the Catholic identity.

Even at those few universities where administrators are keen to hire with their school's religious mission in mind, they can make little progress without faculty cooperation. After decades of hiring almost exclusively on academic pedigree, with questions about a candidate's suitability for the religious mission of the institution having been asked with a wink and a nod, if at all, it is now extremely difficult to ask those faculty members tenured under the old dispensation to take seriously substantive proposals to hire for mission.

Ironies abound—the most dramatic being the way that leading Catholic universities, desperately afraid of being identified with "official" Catholic teachings on sexuality, have abandoned the Catholic intellectual tradition save for some small portion of the Church's teaching on human sexuality. We see this in the Catholic campus debates over the official recognition of gay and lesbian groups, pro-choice groups, and the performance of *The Vagina Monologues*, the result of which at a place like Notre Dame seems to have been to confer on a mediocrity the stature of James Joyce's *Ulysses*.

We are better served in these matters by diversity, rather than homogeneity, in institutions of higher education. But to set out on a different path will mean a willingness to buck the purportedly self-evident claims about what academic excellence means. Both Pope John Paul II and Pope Benedict XVI have made us acutely aware that many Catholic universities are in trouble, not simply because they are no longer Catholic, but because they are no longer universities—arenas for the communal pursuit of truth in a range of disciplines.

CHAPTER 11

Faith and Reason in Catholic Higher Education

MICHAEL DAUPHINAIS
Ave Maria University

DOCTOR HIBBS has provided a most illuminating review of the trajectories within Catholic higher education in America over the past few decades. Moreover, he has drawn helpful attention to the interaction between the liberal arts movements and institutions distinctive of American soil and the specific history of Catholic institutions. The following analysis focuses exclusively on the question of the complementary decline of the liberal arts and Catholic identity within Catholic colleges and universities in the United States, a decline stemming from the separation of faith and reason's access to truth. To put the thesis positively, both liberal arts education and Catholic identity stand or fall with the notion of truth and the human ability to discover and possess that truth.

The disconnect between scholarly inquiry and the possession of truth is evidenced in a 2005 article, "Aquinas and Catholic Universities," by a professor of philosophy at Fordham University.[1] That article presents certain themes from Aquinas concerning teaching, learning, and theology in light of their contribution to contemporary Catholic universities. The article concludes with the following claim:

> In conclusion, though, I have to add that I do not think that Aquinas would favour a ghetto-like approach to Catholic education today. I have been reading and writing about Aquinas for years, and it seems to me to be perfectly clear that he would have had little time

[1] Brian Davies, O.P., "Aquinas and Catholic Universities," *New Blackfriars* 86 (May 2005): 276–90.

> for educational institutions unwilling to engage with views opposed to its basic tenets, or unwilling to expose their students to such views. When George Bernard Shaw visited Washington, D.C., he was told that the Catholic University of America was located in the city. Shaw then said that a Catholic university is a contradiction in terms. I presume that he was expressing an aversion to places in which non-Catholic thinking is not taken seriously. Yet some of the most approvingly quoted authors in Aquinas's writings are not even Christians. So Aquinas clearly thought that people who disagreed with him could help him to learn. And maybe that is one of the chief thoughts he would have wished to bequeath to those concerned with Catholic education today.[2]

Although no one would disagree with the assertion that Aquinas certainly thought we could learn things from those with whom we disagree, it is surely controversial to suggest that Aquinas would have been most at home in the modern secularized university context in which Catholic truth is not formally and institutionally recognized. Since it is unlikely there are schools that actually do not discuss non-Christian or non-Catholic philosophers, I assume that the article's reference to schools unwilling to engage, and expose their students, to those opposed to the Catholic faith has something different in mind.[3] The central assertion addresses the character of Catholic scholarly and educational engagement with the modern world and its philosophies and sciences broadly conceived. The article's final admonition indicates that engagement requires a willingness on the part of Catholic universities actively to bracket (ultimately, not merely initially by the very act of questioning) the conviction that those with whom adherents of the Catholic faith disagree are in fact wrong as regards certain key claims about God and humankind. As a representative of the dominant view within contemporary Catholic higher educational institutions, the article both presupposes and advances an antinomy between the search for truth and resting in truth already possessed.

Here is where Catholic higher education can learn from the consistent magisterial teaching of the Catholic Church on questions of faith and reason over the past century and a half. Within this perspective, Pope John Paul II's 1990 Apostolic Constitution, *Ex Corde Ecclesiae*, should not be read exclusively in terms of its juridical implications but within this broader magisterial tradition. In *Ex Corde Ecclesiae*, Pope John Paul II

---

[2] Ibid., p. 290.

[3] The core curriculum at Ave Maria University, where I serve as both dean and associate professor of theology, does expose students to countless non-Catholic, non-Christian, pre-Christian, anti-Christian, and post-Christian authors.

addressed the dynamic tension between knowledge possessed yet desired: "A Catholic university's privileged task is 'to unite existentially by intellectual effort two orders of reality that too frequently tend to be placed in opposition as though they were antithetical: the search for truth, and the certainty of already knowing the fount of truth.'"[4] By employing the language of "task" and "effort," *Ex Corde Ecclesiae* recognizes the tension between seeking knowledge and security in its position, while refusing the opposition. Were such an opposition to exist, then so would an opposition between the rigorous intellectual inquiry characteristic of a university and the Catholic Church's recognition of herself as the recipient of the deposit of faith from Christ.

Catholic institutions need to begin their educational and scholarly endeavors by confessing "Jesus is Lord" and the rest of the creedal affirmations that bring the believer to know God as he has revealed himself in Jesus Christ.[5] Let me add that I am not accusing the author of the aforementioned article of lacking in the theological virtue of faith proper to a Catholic; I am challenging the assumption that that faith needs to be bracketed in terms of scholarly and educational inquiry. One of the background problems of Catholic higher education in America is the theological and philosophical agnosticism that has plagued modernity. The Magisterium of the Catholic Church has contended against this trajectory since the latter part of the nineteenth century.

As is well known, in 1870, in *Dei Filius*, Vatican I reaffirmed the ability of both faith and reason to know the truth about God: "God, the source and end of all things, can be known with certainty from the consideration of created things, by the natural power of human reason. . . . It was, however, pleasing to his wisdom and goodness to reveal himself and the eternal laws of his will to the human race by another, and that a supernatural, way."[6] Moreover, there was a specific criticism of the tendency to exclude the truth revealed by Christ and communicated through the Church. In a manner prophetic of the postmodernism that would become pervasive in the academy of the second half of the twentieth century, Vatican I connected the intellectual exclusion of Christ to a broader denial of intellectual and moral truths:

---

4 Pope John Paul II, Apostolic Constitution *Ex Corde Ecclesiae* [From the Heart of the Church], 1 (August 15, 1990).

5 See Aquinas's well-known formulation "Now the act of the believer terminates in the reality, not in the proposition. For we formulate propositions only in order to know things by means of them, in faith no less than science" (*Summa Theologiae* II–II, q.1, a.2, ad 2).

6 Vatican I, *Dei Filius*, chap. 2, nos. 1, 2.

> Thereupon there came into being and spread far and wide throughout the world that doctrine of rationalism or naturalism,—utterly opposed to the Christian religion, since this is of supernatural origin,—which spares no effort to bring it about that Christ, who alone is our lord and savior, is shut out from the minds of people and the moral life of nations. Thus they would establish what they call the rule of simple reason or nature. The abandonment and rejection of the Christian religion, and the denial of God and his Christ, has plunged the minds of many into the abyss of pantheism, materialism and atheism, and the consequence is that they strive to destroy rational nature itself, to deny any criterion of what is right and just, and to overthrow the very foundations of human society.[7]

Continuing this battle against modern agnosticism, in his 1907 *Pascendi Dominici Gregis* (On the Doctrines of the Modernists) St. Pope Pius X identified the philosophical roots of modernism to lie in agnosticism, such that divine truth cannot be received into our minds. As a consequence the Catholic religion is not objectively revealed, but rather springs from man's own sensibility due to what *Pascendi* terms a vital immanence. The authority of the Church therefore was not dependent on the revelation of God in Jesus Christ; instead, the Church's authority rather derived from the consent of the individual consciences of the members of the Church.

These themes were reiterated even more strongly in some ways in Pope John Paul II's encyclical *Fides et Ratio*. There he drew attention to the beautiful image that faith and reason were the two wings by which the human person ascended to truth. Yet, by the end of the twentieth century, not only faith, but also reason had been become largely suspect as a means for attaining the truth about the human person.

Cardinal Ratzinger addressed a similar crisis of truth in faith in the 2000 Declaration "*Dominus Iesus*," whose central theme was dedicated to reaffirming the universality and uniqueness of Jesus Christ and the Church in salvation. Similar to Vatican I, 130 years before, "*Dominus Iesus*" begins with a profession of the Nicene-Constantinopolitan Creed that Catholics profess each Sunday at Mass. In Cardinal Ratzinger's Conclave Homily (immediately prior to his papal election), he opposed the concept of the dictatorship of relativism to faith as creedal and therefore knowable.

> Having a clear faith, based upon the Creed of the Church, is often labeled today as a fundamentalism. Whereas, relativism, which is letting oneself be tossed and "swept along by every wind of teaching", looks like the only attitude (acceptable) to today's standards. We are

[7] Ibid., chap. 1, no. 7.

> moving towards *a dictatorship of relativism* which does not recognize anything as for certain and which has as its highest goal one's own ego and one's own desires (italics added).[8]

In his *Pilgrim Fellowship of Faith*, Cardinal Ratzinger correlates faith and certainty:

> In reality, for the believing Christian the words "I believe" articulate a particular kind of certainty—one that is in many respects a higher degree of certainty than that of science yet one that does indeed carry within it the dynamics of "shadow and image", the dynamic of the "not yet". . . . We live faith, not as a hypothesis, but as the certainty on which our life is based. If two people regard their love merely as a hypothesis that is constantly in need of new verification, they destroy love in that way.[9]

Faith brings with it a kind of certainty, a certainty that makes possible the bond of *caritas* between the faithful and God.

Yet, as we have seen, the view that faith is properly joined with certainty has not been accepted throughout much within contemporary Catholic higher education in America. Consider the following comments about faith and doubt from President Barack Obama's 2009 commencement speech delivered at the University of Notre Dame: "Hold firm to your faith and allow it to guide you on your journey. In other words, stand as a lighthouse. But remember, too, that you can be a crossroads. Remember, too, that the ultimate irony of faith is that it necessarily admits doubt. It's the belief in things not seen. It's beyond our capacity as human beings to know with certainty what God has planned for us or what He asks of us."[10] Although this was not a speech by a Catholic educator, the fact that it was warmly received with a standing ovation by students, faculty, and school officials indicates a strong resonance. Faith here excludes certainty. In fact, it is this very view of faith excluding certainty that has led to numerous Catholic institutions of higher education inviting pro-abortion commencement speakers, despite the directives and statements to the contrary from bishops.

---

[8] Joseph Cardinal Ratzinger, "Homily of His Emimence Cardinal Joseph Ratzinger, Dean of the College of Cardinals," April 18, 2005, www.vatican.va/gpII/documents/homily-pro-eligendo-pontifice_20050418_en.html.

[9] Cardinal Ratzinger, *Pilgrim Fellowship of Faith* (San Francisco: Ignatius Press, 2005), pp. 19–20.

[10] President Barack Obama, commencement address, University of Notre Dame, May 17, 2009.

To understand the abandonment of so many Catholic schools from their Catholic identity and the mission of liberal education or their resistance to the guidance of the Church expressed in *Ex Corde Ecclesiae,* one must consider that the loss of the conviction that truth is knowable by faith and reason drove many to redefine themselves in terms that were compatible with the broader agnostic convictions of the age. There were many other models of universities in America that could be imitated. The models of offering professional advancement to young people, technical training and specialization, or of research institutions could be pursued independent of a liberal education centered on truth. These other models are not necessarily opposed to truth; and they have been a part of the work of universities from the days of medieval Paris to Newman's Ireland. Yet, the engagement with professional preparation and academic research to the exclusion of the liberal arts and the truth of the Catholic faith leads to a different kind of institution; the central questions about human existence no longer animate its ethos. Conversely, the center of liberal education when vigorously present can provide an impetus for the properly human development of professional programs and research centers and institutes.

The success of Catholic higher education, nevertheless, cannot be determined solely by the adherence of a particular institution's members to the Catholic faith. As the Church has proposed from Vatican I through *Fides et Ratio* and now through Pope Benedict's Regensburg lecture ("Faith, Reason and the University"), the affirmation that faith can yield truth and thus certainty goes hand in hand with the affirmation that human reason can know truths about God, man, and the world. Thus truth becomes the center of the project of liberal education within the Catholic context—a truth possessed yet desired. Thus the truth is not absolutely known, for if the source of truth lies in the infinite Creator, then all truth has an unfathomable character, as Josef Pieper has observed. Thus an institution's Catholic identity is not only necessary to sustain its mission of liberal education because of the conviction of the unity of truth; conversely, the engagement with liberal education uniquely sustains an institution's Catholic identity.

In terms of faculty, it is well known that *Ex Corde Ecclesiae* requires the majority of the faculty be Catholic. This is sometimes pilloried as incompatible with academic excellence, sometimes misunderstood as not fully hospitable to the non-Catholic faculty member. If the recognition of truth as both knowable and unfathomable by faith and reason is the center of liberal education, then the distinctive contribution that a Catholic institution of higher education can make depends upon the faculty of that institution affirming the centrality of the search for truth both as something known and desired. Thus it is more than whether the faculty in a given discipline are practicing Catholics. The deeper issue is the extent to which they conceive of their teaching and research stemming from a relationship to the truth: both the truth as revealed in the Person of Jesus Christ and as discovered through the application of reason to the central questions of human existence. The requirement that a majority of faculty be Catholic encourages the realization of this conviction. Moreover, it sets a context and a criterion for the introduction of non-Catholic faculty members into the faculty. Non-Catholic faculty members should be able to affirm the existence of truth and its unity and pursue it within the context of natural reason as well as their faith tradition.

I would also like to make a suggestion for a development within *Ex Corde Ecclesiae*'s guidelines that the majority of the faculty should be Catholic. Many of the decisions within a university are made by the different disciplinary departments, not by the entire faculty. These decisions would include the curriculum within each major, hiring decisions, and evaluations of student learning and achievements, at least at their initial level before oversight by the larger faculty and administration of the university. Given the level of disciplinary specialization necessary to a university-level education, this is largely as it should be. Nonetheless, if the only criterion is that more than 50 percent of the overall faculty be Catholic, this could easily result in a situation in which many departments have little or no Catholic representation or leadership. Thus it would seem more appropriate to require that the majority of the faculty be Catholic within each department, school, or decision-making body within the university. Not only does this seem a more secure way to sustain the Catholic identity of the school over time; it also allows the different disciplines to maintain a more proper relative autonomy. Each department then seeks the proper way within its discipline to seek the truth as known from its own methodologies, in conversation with other disciplines, and finally as enlightened by revelation. The connection to the liberal arts mission, rooted in the truth known by faith and reason, thus is not something imposed from the outside by nondisciplinary specialists but comes forth from the departments in dialogue with the rest of the university.

Finally, I would like to close with an observation about where we are today. We might consider a parallel in the Church's stance in the political realm. Over the past few centuries, the Church grappled with the loss of historically Catholic nations. As Cardinal George summarized in an excellent manner, after the initial condemnation of emergent democracies as religiously neutral, the Church in Vatican II acknowledged that constitutional democracies were valid forms of political association. This entailed, of course, recognizing that the majority of Catholic confessional states had simply ceased to exist at least in terms of the political regime. The same thing may well be the case for Catholic confessional institutions of higher education. Many have simply ceased being so. When we survey the loss of so many Catholic confessional states over the past few centuries, we do well to focus on the present good we can do within our current regime.

Crying over the French monarchy seems ill conceived at this point in time. Similarly, the rationale for this present diagnosis of the loss of Catholic identity and liberal education at so many Catholic schools is not lamentation. When we discover that the loss of religion and the loss of liberal education went hand in hand, we should work to keep the Catholic faith and liberal education united during this third millennium. At times, Catholic intellectuals have found ways of pursuing liberal education under a Catholic inspiration at times within institutions either secular or of a non-Catholic Christian affiliation. In other cases, Catholic institutions have begun seeking a renewal of fidelity to their Catholic mission and thus their liberal arts core. And, a number of institutions in the American context have been founded in the past several decades with the explicit purpose of sustaining and fostering the commitment to the Catholic mission, one that necessarily includes reflections on the truth of man, the world, and God.

About the Contributors

Archbishop Charles J. Chaput, OFM, DD, Archbishop of Philadelphia, joined the Order of Friars Minor Capuchin, St. Augustine Province, in 1965. He was ordained Bishop of Rapid City, South Dakota, on July 26, 1988. Pope John Paul II appointed him Archbishop of Denver on February 18, 1997, and Pope Benedict XVI appointed him Archbishop of Philadelphia on July 19, 2011. He earned a Master of Arts in Religious Education from Capuchin College in Washington, D.C., in 1970, and a Master of Arts in Theology from the University of San Francisco in 1971. As a member of the Prairie Band Potawatomi Tribe, Archbishop Chaput was the second Native American to be ordained bishop in the United States, and the first Native American archbishop. He is author of two books: *Living the Catholic Faith: Rediscovering the Basics* (Servant, 2001) and *Render unto Caesar: Serving the Nation by Living Our Catholic Beliefs in Political Life* (Doubleday, 2008); and numerous talks, articles and pastoral letters. His writings, discourses, and homilies are available at www.archphila.org/archbishop-chaput/index.htm and www.archden.org/archbishop.

Michael Dauphinais, Ph.D. is Dean of Faculty and Associate Professor of Theology. Together with Dr. Matthew Levering, he has co-edited *Reading John with St. Thomas Aquinas: Theological Exegesis and Speculative Theology* (Catholic University of America Press, 2006); *Reading Romans with St. Thomas Aquinas* (CUA Press, 2012); with Dr. Levering he also coauthored *Knowing the Love of Christ: An Introduction to the Theology of St. Thomas Aquinas* (Notre Dame University Press, 2005) and *Holy People, Holy Land: A Theological Introduction to the Bible* (Brazos Press, 2008). His theological research includes moral theology, Christology, and the theology of revelation.

Dr. Dauphinais holds the degrees of B.S.E. from Duke University, M.T.S. from Duke Divinity School, and Ph.D. from the University of Notre Dame. He is a co-director of the Center for Catholic Theological Renewal and a member of the Academy of Catholic Theology.

Francis Cardinal George, O.M.I., Archbishop of Chicago, entered the Missionary Oblates of Mary Immaculate in 1957. He obtained an M.A. in philosophy at Catholic University of America, and an M.A. in theology at the University of Ottawa; he obtained a Ph.D. in American philosophy at Tulane University. He also obtained a Doctorate in Sacred Theology from the Pontifical Urbana University of Rome in 1988. Pope John Paul II appointed him Bishop of Yakima, Washington, in 1990. He served as bishop there for five and a half years. Then he was appointed the ninth Archbishop of Portland, Oregon, in 1996 and a year later John Paul II appointed him the eighth Archbishop of Chicago, and in 1998 elevated him to the Sacred College of Cardinals. He has published most recently *The Difference God Makes: A Catholic Vision of Faith, Communion, and Culture* (Herder & Herder, 2009). He has over thirty scholarly articles in journals and books. Cardinal George is a member of four Vatican Congregations, two Pontifical Commissions, and one Pontifical Council. He serves on many commissions in the United States Conference of Catholic Bishops, and was its elected Vice-President from 2004–2007, and President of the United States Conference of Catholic Bishops in 2008.

Marc D. Guerra, Ph.D., is associate professor of theology at Ave Maria University in Ave Maria, Florida. He is the author of *Christians as Political Animals: Taking the Measure of Modernity and Modern Democracy*, and editor of *Reason, Revelation and Human Affairs; Jerusalem, Athens, and Rome*; and *Pope Benedict XVI and the Politics of Modernity* (Forthcoming Routledge). Guerra is also co-editor of *The Science of Modern Virtue: Essays on Descartes, Darwin, and Locke* (Forthcoming Northern Illinois University Press). He is currently writing a book titled *Vatican II and the Dialectics of Modernity: 50 Years Later*. His essays on the relation of faith and reason, Christianity and political philosophy, Augustine and Aquinas, and human dignity and bioethics have appeared in *Religious Studies and Theology, The Political Science Reviewer, Logos, Interpretation, Gregorianum, Society, First Things*, and *Perspectives on Political Science*.

Thomas Hibbs, Ph.D., is Dean of the Honors College and Distinguished Professor of Ethics and Culture at Baylor University. With doctoral degrees from the University of Dallas and the University of Notre Dame, Dr. Hibbs taught at Boston College for 13 years, where he was full professor and department chair in philosophy. He has published scholarly books on Aquinas, including *Dialectic and Narrative in Aquinas: An Interpretation of the Summa Contra Gentiles* (University of Notre Dame Press, 1995); *Virtue's Splendor: Wisdom, Prudence, and the Human Good* (Fordham University Press, 2001) , and a book on popular culture entitled *Shows About Nothing* (Spence Publications, 2000, new edition with Baylor University Press, 2012). Hibbs has published scholarly articles on MacIntyre and Aquinas (*Review of Politics*), on Anselm (*Anselm Studies*), and on Pascal (*International Philosophical Quarterly*). He also has written on film, culture, books, and higher education in *Books and Culture, Christianity Today, First Things, New Atlantis, The Dallas Morning News, The National Review, The Weekly Standard, and The Chronicle of Higher Education, Wall Street Journal.*

Rev. Matthew L. Lamb, Dr. Theol., is Professor and Chair of the Department of Theology at Ave Maria University. He was a monk at the Trappist monastery of Our Lady of the Holy Spirit in Conyers, Georgia and plans on returning to a contemplative monastery after teaching. He received a Licentiate in theology (S.T.L.) from the Pontifical Gregorian University of Rome, Italy. His Doctorate in Theology (Dr. Theol.) "Summa cum laude" was done at the Westfälische Wilhelms Universität, Münster, Germany in 1974. He is a Roman Catholic priest belonging to the Archdiocese of Milwaukee, Wisconsin. He received an honorary doctorate from the Franciscan University of Steubenville in 2002. He has taught in the Theology Department at Marquette University, and Boston College. He has lectured at universities in Europe and North and Central America. His books include *Eternity, Time and the Life of Wisdom* (Sapientia Press, 2007); *Thomas Aquinas's Commentary on Ephesians* (Magi Books, 1966; new edition 2012). *History, Method and Theology* (Scholars Press, 1978); *Solidarity with Victims* (Crossroads, 1982). He edited *Creativity and Method: Essays in Honor of Bernard Lonergan* (Marquette University Press, 1981) and co-edited *Vatican II: Renewal Within Tradition* (Oxford University Press, 2008). He has published over a hundred and forty-five articles in books and journals.

Peter Augustine Lawler, Ph.D., is Dana Professor of Government at Berry College. His books include: *Aliens in America: The Strange Truth about Our Souls* (ISI Books, 2002); *Postmodernism Rightly Understood* (Rowman & Littlefield Publishers, 1999); *Stuck with Virtue: The American Individual and Our Biotechnological Future* (ISI Books 2005); *Homeless and At Home in America* (St. Augustine's Press, 2007). He also edited with

Robert Schaefer *American Political Rhetoric* (Fourth Edition edition with Rowman & Littlefield, 2000). He is executive editor of the quarterly journal, *Perspectives on Political Science* and also serves on the editorial boards of several journals. In 2004, Lawler was appointed to President Bush's Council on Bioethics. Dr. Peter Lawler and Dr. Marc Guerra have received grants from The Templeton Foundation and the University of Chicago to engage in ongoing projects studying the interface of science, theology, and philosophy with special attention to bio-technology and bio-ethics. Their project on a new science of virtue was one of twenty selected out of over seven hundred applications.

William Cardinal Levada, Prefect of the Congregation for the Doctrine of the Faith, was ordained a priest in 1961 and received his S.T.D. "magna cum laude" from the Pontifical Gregorian University in 1971, teaching theology at St. John's School of Theology. In 1983 he was appointed an auxiliary bishop of Los Angeles. In 1986 he became the Archbishop of Portland, and served as the only American bishop on the Editorial Committee of the Vatican Commission for the *Catechism of the Catholic Church.* In 1995 Archbishop Levada succeeded Archbishop John Quinn as seventh Archbishop of San Francisco. In 2000 he was appointed by the Vatican as a Member of the Congregation for the Doctrine of the Faith. Five years later Pope Benedict XVI announced Archbishop Levada to be his successor as Prefect of the Congregation for the Doctrine of the Faith. In the Consistory of March 24, 2006, the Archbishop was appointed to the Sacred College of Cardinals.

Daniel J. Mahoney, Ph.D. is Chair and Distinguished Professor of Political Science at Assumption College. He received his M.A. and Ph.D. in Political Science at the Catholic University of America. He is the author of over one hundred book introductions, articles, and book reviews that have appeared in a wide range of scholarly and public journals. His writings have appeared in French, Italian, Hungarian, and Portuguese translation. Dr. Mahoney's publications include: *The Liberal Political Science of Raymond Aron* (Rowman & Littlefield, 1992; a French edition appeared in 1998); *De Gaulle: Statesmanship, Grandeur, and Modern Democracy* (Praeger, 1996; revised paperback edition, Transaction Publishers, 2001); *Aleksandr Solzhenitsyn: The Ascent From Ideology* (Rowman & Littlefield, 2001; a French edition published in October 2007); *Bertrand de Jouvenel: The Conservative Liberal and the Illusions of Modernity* (ISI Books, 2005); and he is coeditor with Edward Ericson, Jr., *The Solzhenitsyn Reader: New and Essential Writings, 1947–2005.* (ISI Books, 2006). Mahoney has been a visiting professor at a number of universities including Harvard University, The Paris-Sorbonne University, Boston College, etc. He has made well over one hundred presentations at professional and public conferences. In 1999 Professor Mahoney was the recipient of the prestigious *Prix Raymond Aron.* He is associate editor of *Perspectives on Political Science* and book review editor of *Society.*

Michael Novak served as United States Ambassador to the United Nations Commission on Human Rights in 1981 and 1982 and led the U.S. delegation to the Conference on Security and Cooperation in Europe in 1986. He is now a Distinguished Lecturer at Ave Maria University in He is the author of more than twenty-five books on the philosophy and theology of culture, Novak is most widely known for his book *The Spirit of Democratic Capitalism* (Madison Books, 1982 revised edition 1990) that has been translated into many languages and was influential with the Solidarity movement in Poland. Most recently he has published: *All Nature is a Sacramental Fire: Moments of Beauty, Joy, and Sorrow* (St. Augustine Press, 2011); with William Simon *Living the Call: An Introduction to the Lay Vocation* (Encounter Books 2011); *No One Sees God: The Dark Night of Atheists and Believers* (Doubleday, 2008); *Washington's God* with Jana Novak (Basic Books, 2006); *On Two Wings: Humble Faith and Common Sense at the American Founding* (Encounter Books, 2003). He has received honorary doctorates and in 1994 he was awarded the Templeton Prize for Progress in Religion, which included a million-dollar purse awarded at Buckingham Palace.

George Weigel is the William E. Simon Chair in Catholic Studies and Distinguished Senior Fellow at the Ethics & Public Policy Center. He was educated at St. Mary's Seminary College (B.A.) and at the University of St. Michael's College in Toronto (M.A.). In 1984–1985 Weigel was a fellow of the Woodrow Wilson International Center for Scholars in Washington, D.C. There, he wrote *Tranquillitas Ordinis: The Present Failure and Future Promise of American Catholic Thought on War and Peace* (Oxford University Press, 1987). He is the author or editor of nineteen other books, including *The Final Revolution: The Resistance Church and the Collapse of Communism* (Oxford, 1992); *The Truth of Catholicism: Ten Controversies Explored* (HarperCollins, 2001); *The Courage To Be Catholic: Crisis, Reform, and the Future of the Church* (Basic Books, 2002); *Letters to a Young Catholic* (Basic, 2004); *The Cube and the Cathedral: Europe, America, and Politics Without God* (Basic, 2005); *God's Choice: Pope Benedict XVI and the Future of the Catholic Church* (Harper Collins, 2005); *Faith, Reason, and the War*

Against Jihadism (Doubleday, 2007); and *Against the Grain: Christianity and Democracy, War and Peace* (Crossroad, 2008). He has published a major study of the life, thought, and action of Pope John Paul II: *Witness to Hope: The Biography of Pope John Paul II* (Harper Collins, 1999), followed by *The End and the Beginning: Pope John Paul II—The Victory of Freedom, the Last Years, the Legacy* (Doubleday, 2010). His books are translated into many languages. Weigel has been awarded twelve honorary doctorates, the papal cross *Pro Ecclesia et Pontifice*, and the *Gloria Artis* Gold Medal by the Republic of Poland.

Index

CPSIA information can be obtained at www.ICGtesting.com
Printed in the USA
BVOW031217071012

302328BV00005B/2/P

9 781932 589634